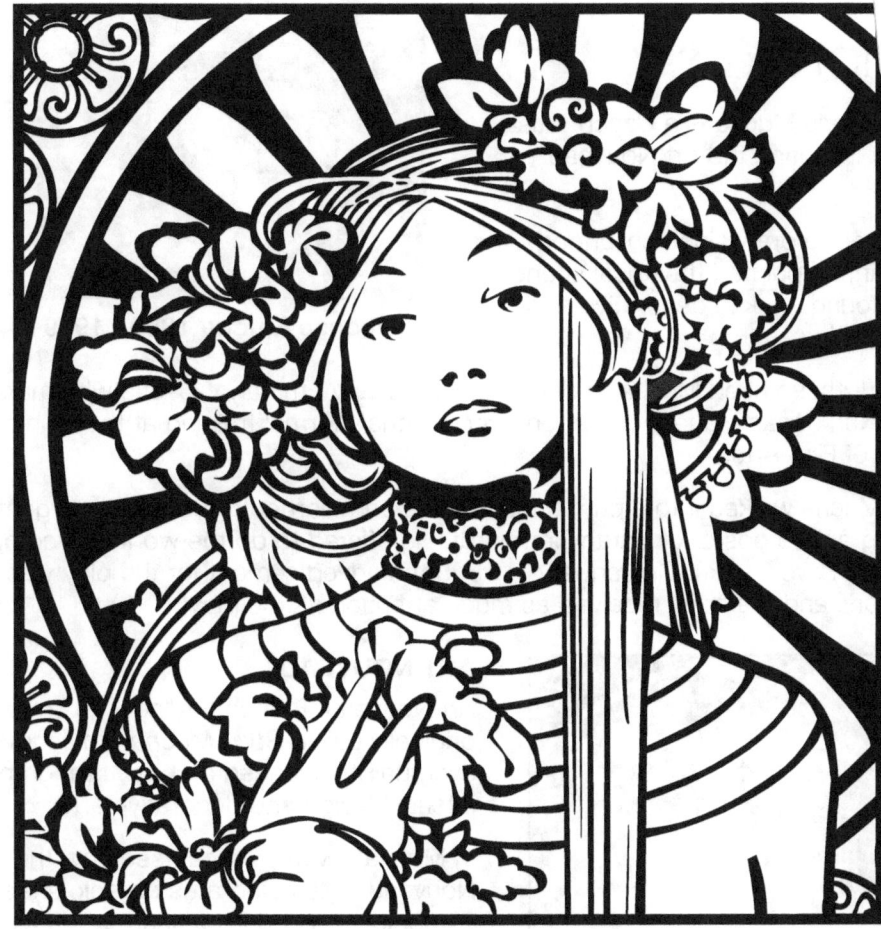

ART NOUVEAU
Fine Art Coloring Book

Art Nouveau Coloring Book / Art History

Jennifer Kozlansky

Published 2015, 2016 by FineArtColoring.com

*Special thanks to my dearest husband Scott
and my wonderful parents Ben & Lou Ann.*

COLORING EVENTS
Visit FineArtColoring.com to learn how to host the best coloring event!
Coloring events are perfect for fundraising, publicity, awareness, cultural centers, art studios, and reunions.

Alphonse

Alphonse Maria Mucha is a Czech artist, known for inventing the Art Nouveau Movement.

Mucha loved to draw since childhood. As a young man, he painted theatrical scenery and also found work in decorative and portrait painting.

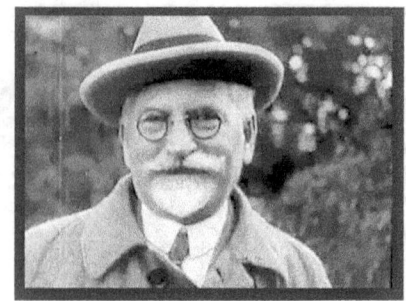

Alphonse Mucha 1860 - 1939

Count Karl Khuen hired Mucha to decorate Hrušovany Emmahof Castle with murals. Good ol' Karl became a fan, and sponsored Mucha's formal training at the Munich Academy of Fine Arts.

In 1894, Mucha walked into a print shop in Paris and learned there was an urgent need for a lithographed poster of Sarah Bernhardt. He offered to do the work and completed the project in two weeks. On January 1, 1895 the advertisement for the play was posted all over Paris and the artist received as much attention as the play!

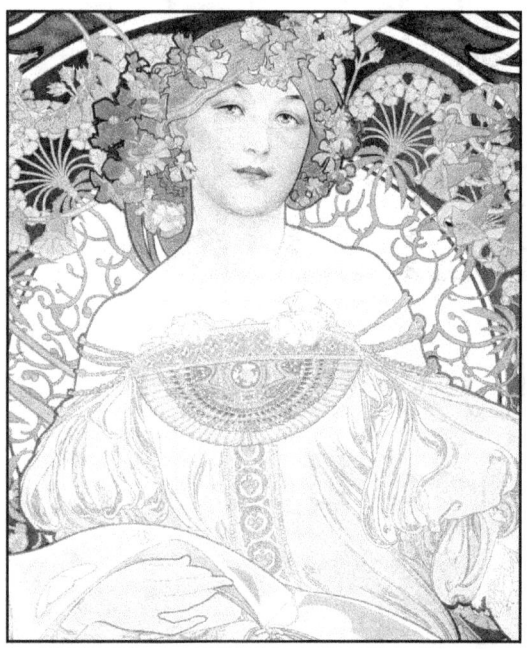

F. Champenois is a masterpiece created as an advertisment for Mucha's primary printer and lithographer.

ART NOUVEAU

Art Nouveau, French for "new art", was originally called _Style Mucha_. This movement eventually influenced architecture, graphic arts, interior design and decorative arts.

In Mucha's work, we can see how the Art Nouveau style celebrates organic shapes. Sweeping, curved lines seem to dance off each other against lush patterns of flora.

He varied the thickness and darkness of his line to draw your attention to a particular area. He then distributed these areas carefully throughout the painting so the viewer's eye is moved through the work.

MUCHA'S FINE ART

The Slav Epic was considered by Mucha to be his fine art masterpiece. It is a series of twenty paintings, up to eight meters across, depicting the history of the Czech and Slavic people. He completed the work in 1928. It can be seen today at the National Gallery's Veletržní Palace.

NAZIS ARE MEAN

The 1930's saw a change in politics. Mucha's artwork, particularly the work focusing on Slav nationalism, fell out of favor. The local press declared his works reactionary and, when German troops entered Czechoslovakia in the spring of 1939, the aging artist was one of the first to be arrested and interrogated by the Gestapo. This harsh treatment was too much for Mucha, and he developed pneumonia. Despite his release, his health declined and he died on July 14,1939 of a lung infection.

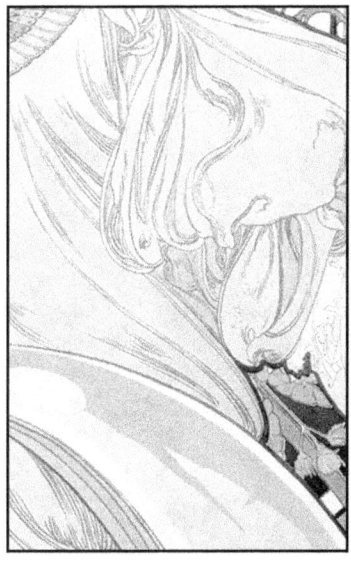

HOW ARTISTS CAN LEARN FROM MUCHA

Mucha was clearly a genius, especially when it came to line quality. So when you sketch on your own, always pay attention to your lines. Note how Mucha often groups multiple lines in certain areas, then reduces the number of lines, the weight of the line, or both, in other areas.

This gives the object visual weight, without the use of shading. It also results in more visual interest. If the line is the same weight throughout, it flattens the piece.

Draw from artists like Mucha and, most importantly, draw from life. Play around with line weight as you sketch your cat, a vase of flowers, anything and everything in real life.

Do you love to color or draw? Looking to improve your results? Sign up for free to The Coloring Academy™ at FineArtColoring.com for videos, discounts, worksheets, and better materials that will make your next coloring project even more beautiful.

Jennifer

Hello Coloristas! I love art. I've studied Illustration at Ringling College of Art, and had 20 years in this field.

But what I love more is to champion other's talent in any form. That is my real passion. So when I discovered the coloring world I found a place I could cheer others on as they created. And to see my own work colored? It was the best feeling I've ever had as an artist.

I call the coloring phenomenon: *"The ultimate collaboration between artists"* and I am fully committed to the talented colorists that make our work come alive every day.

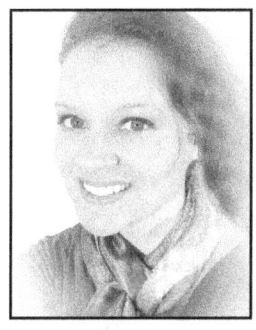

Jennifer Kozlansky

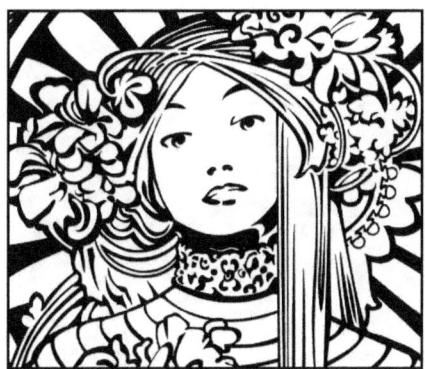

Find Jennifer's latest works, Personalized Get Well Gifts and Color Party Kits on FineArtColoring.com

I showed that commitment by founding FineArtColoring.com. A site that provides the better materials and information it takes that make the colorist's experience more enjoyable and her final piece even more beautiful.

The site is for both casual fans of coloring and dedicated Coloristas to enjoy all sorts of coloring goodness. A gorgeous line of coloring products gives anyone a creative way to say 'Get Well Soon' or celebrate with a gorgeous Color Party Kit.

I live with my husband in Pennsylvania, where I enjoy watching wildlife, travel, volunteering and spending time with my family.

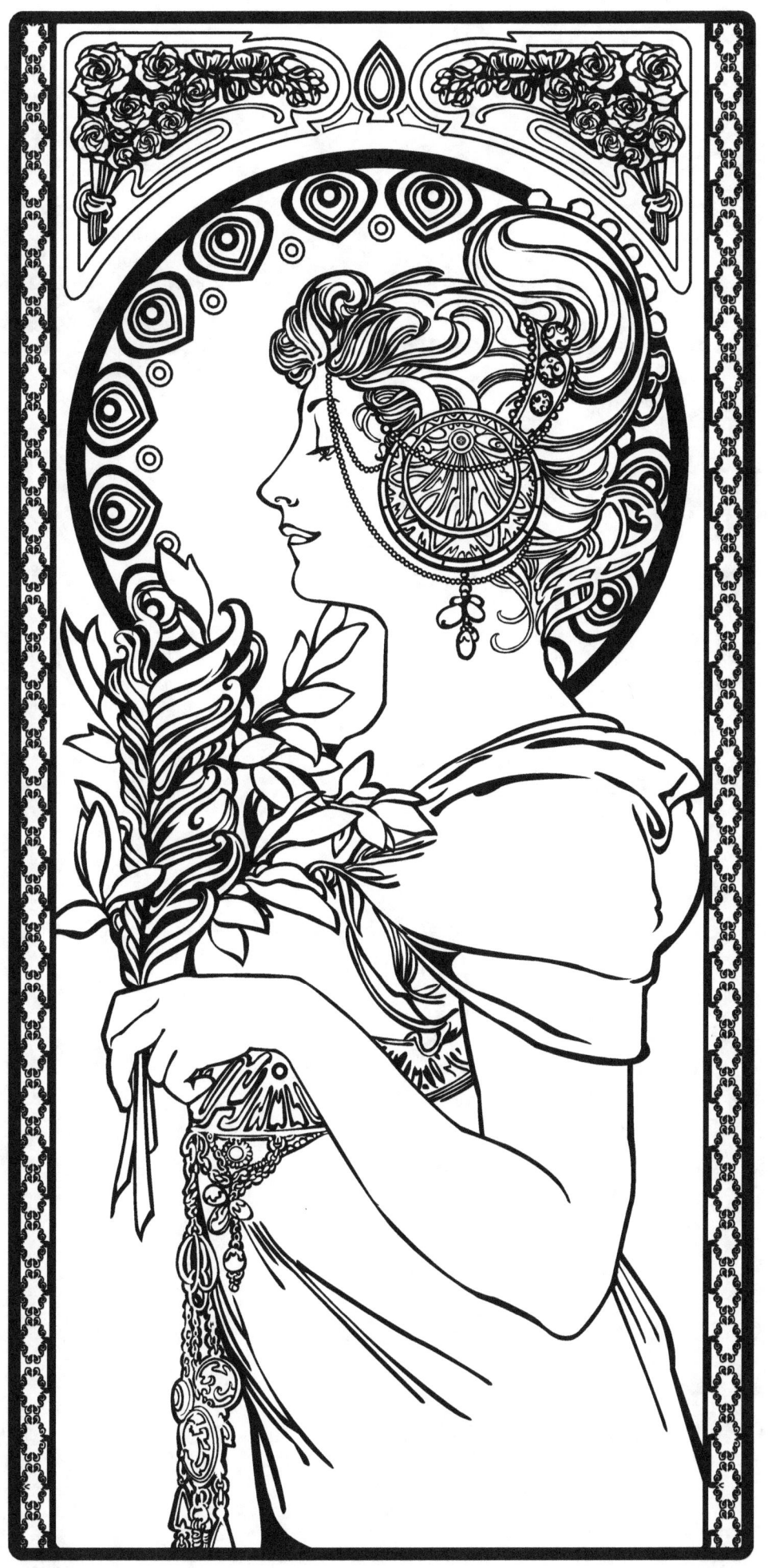

La Plume, 1899 Alphonse Mucha

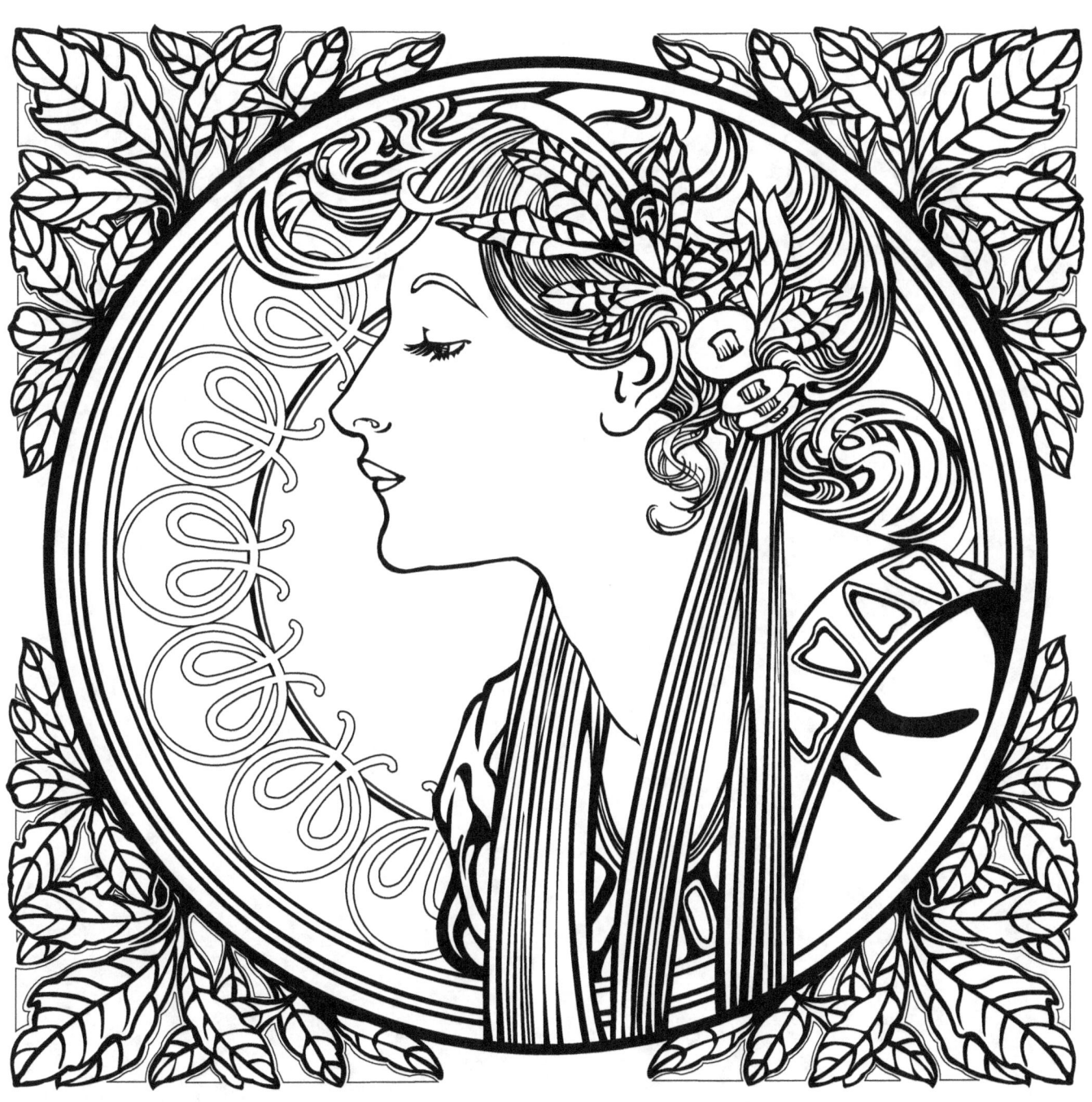

Laurel, 1901 Alphonse Mucha

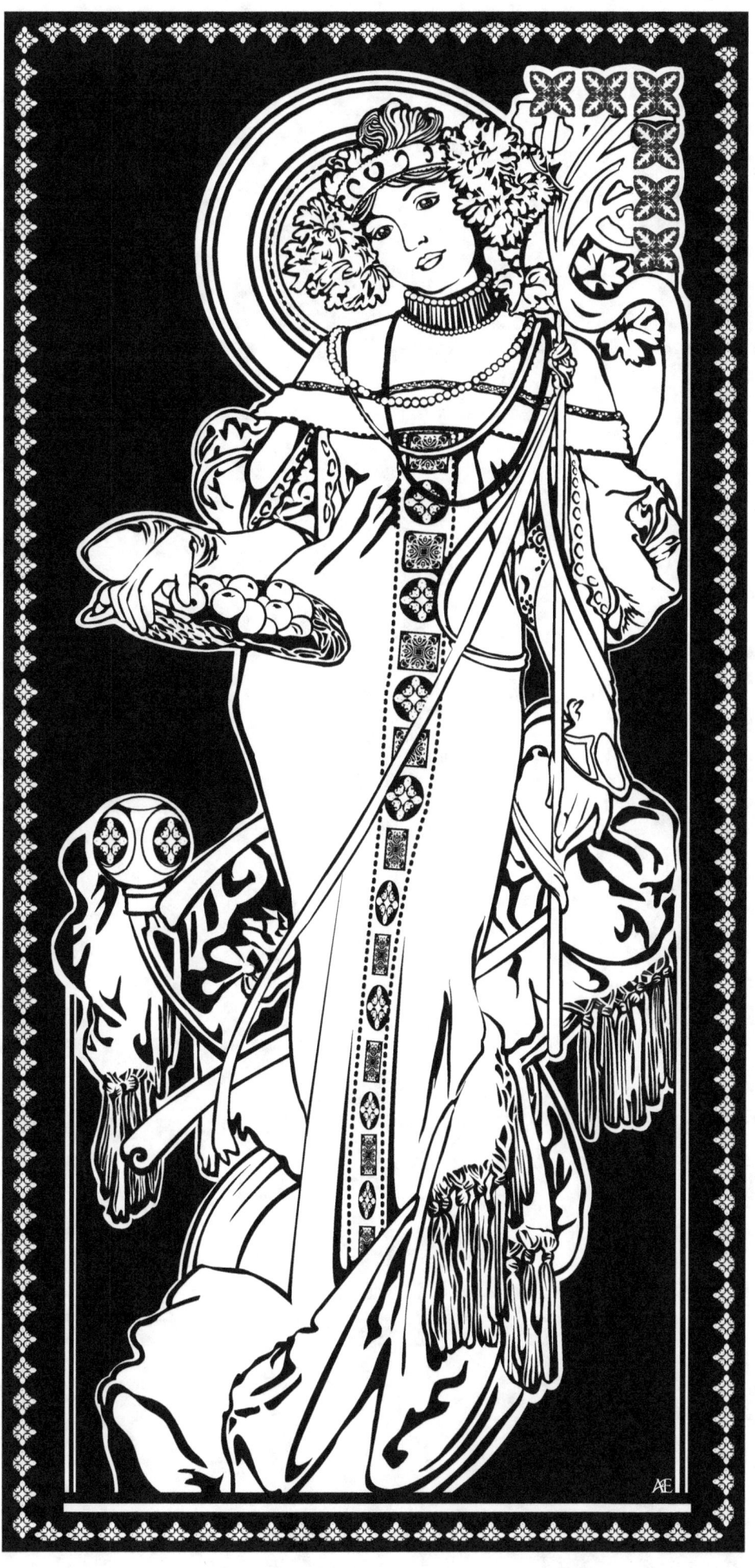

AUTUMN, 1903 ALPHONSE MUCHA

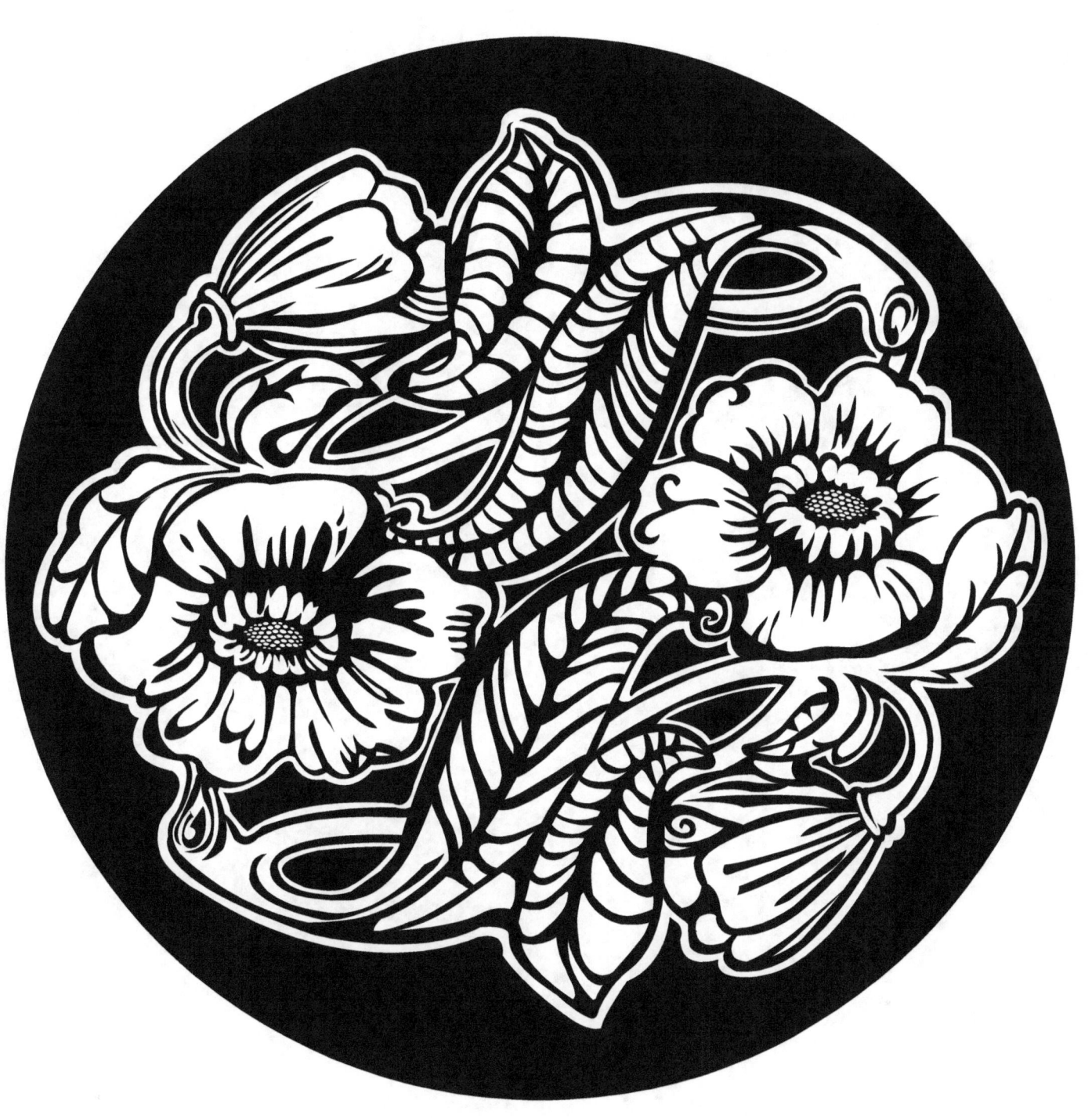

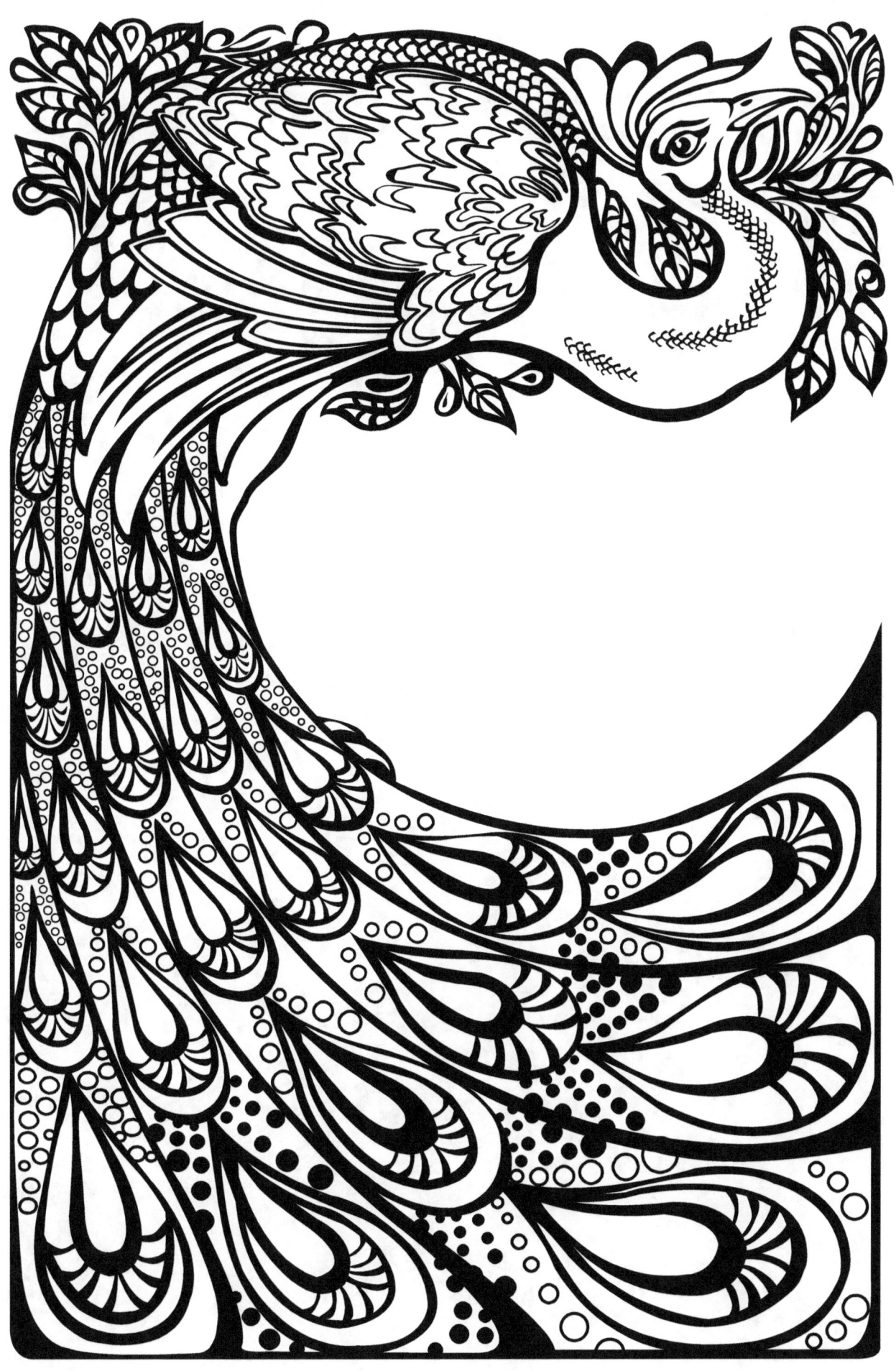

Peacock Book Cover, 1896 A. Turbayne

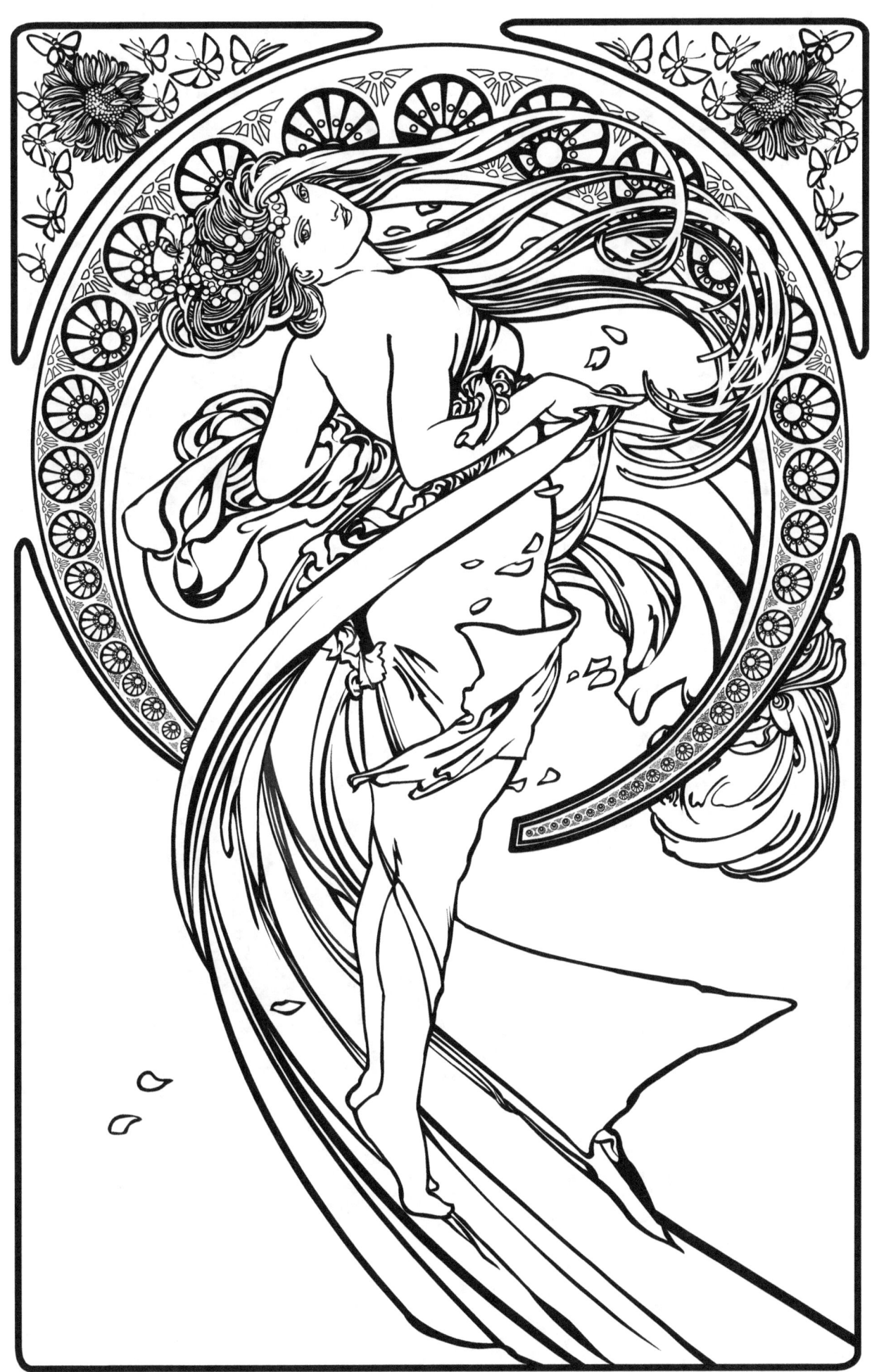

Dance, 1898 Alphonse Mucha

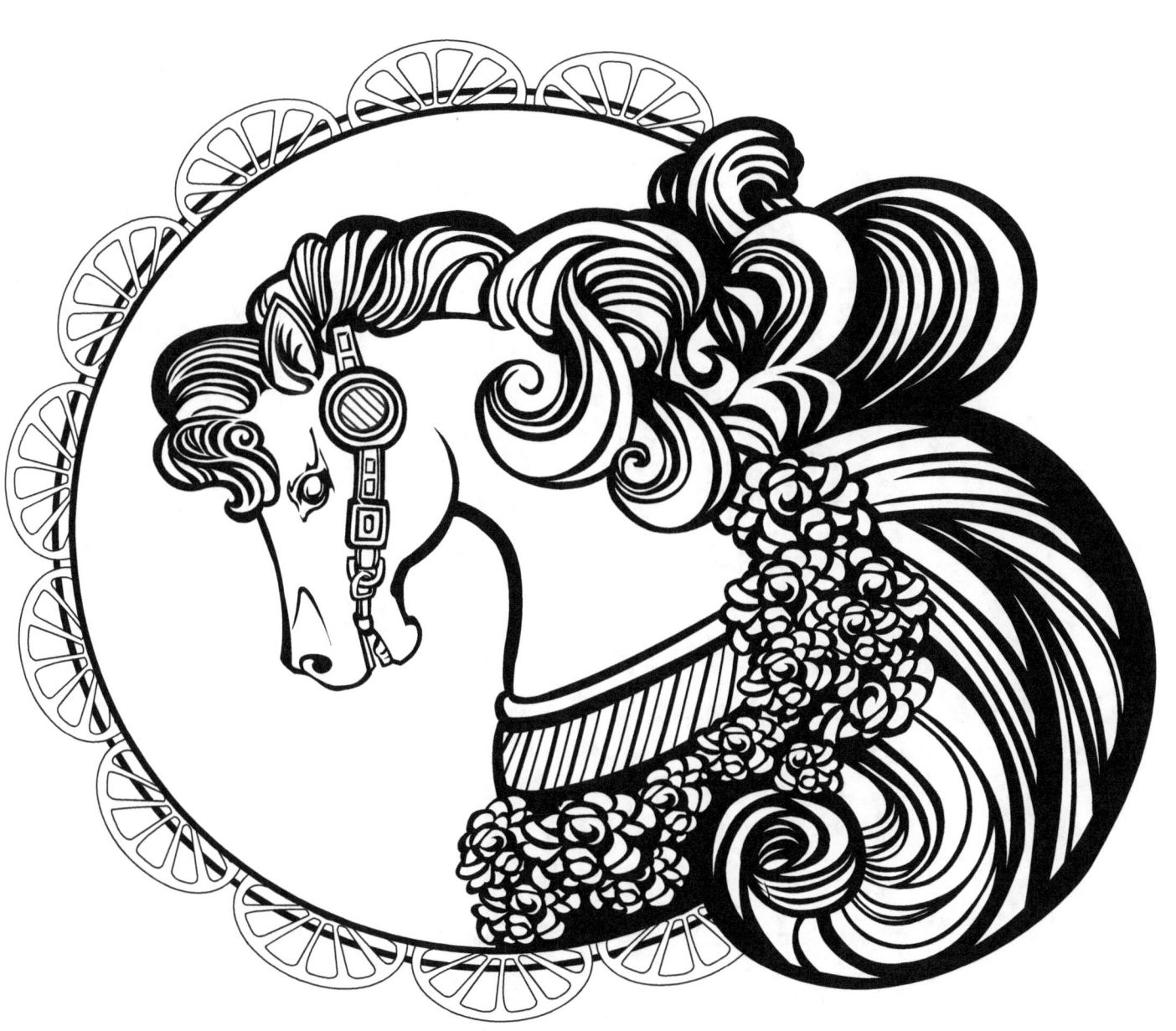

DAHLIA HORSE, 2015 JENNIFER KOZLANSKY

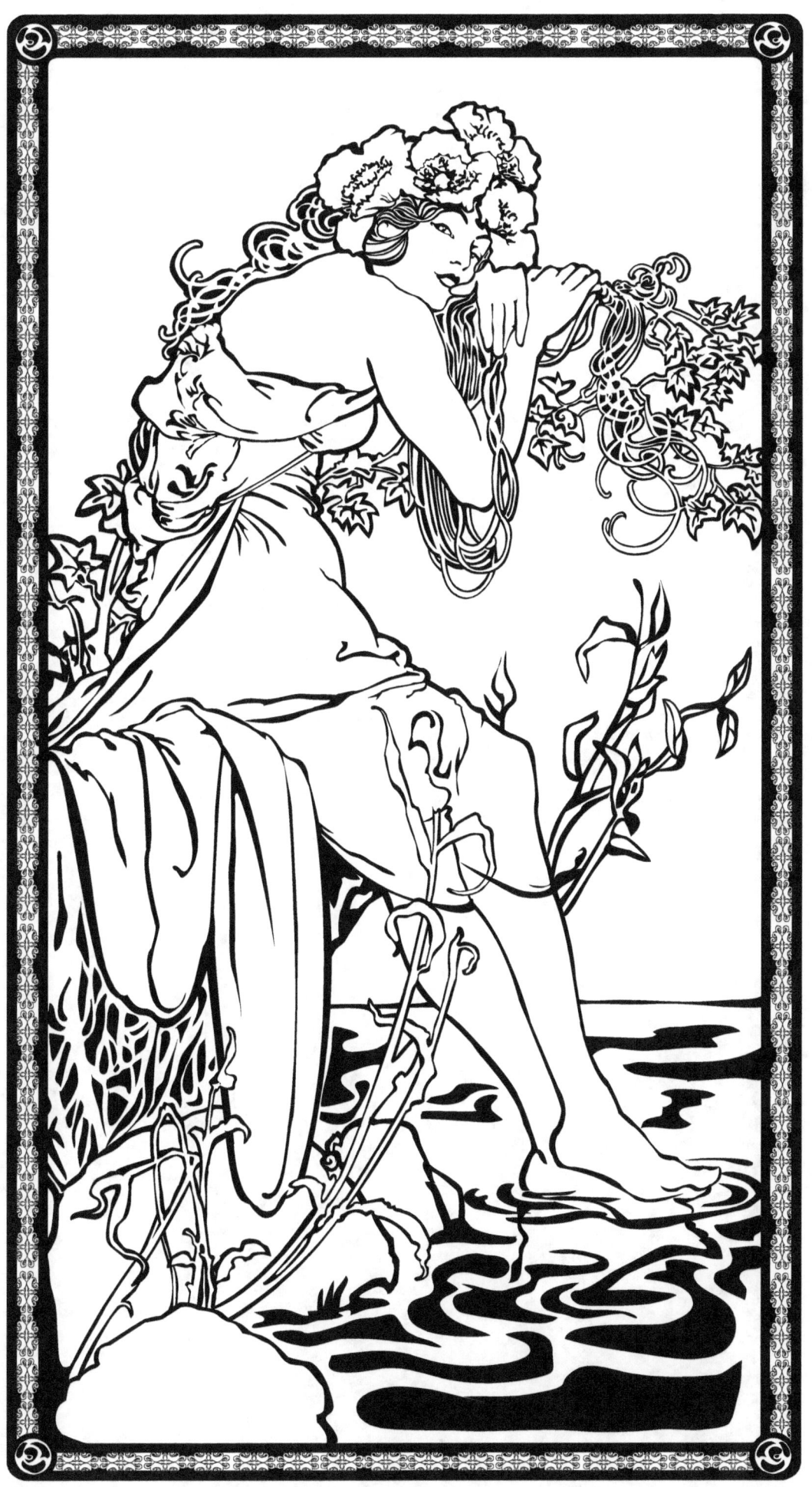

Summer, 1896 Alphonse Mucha

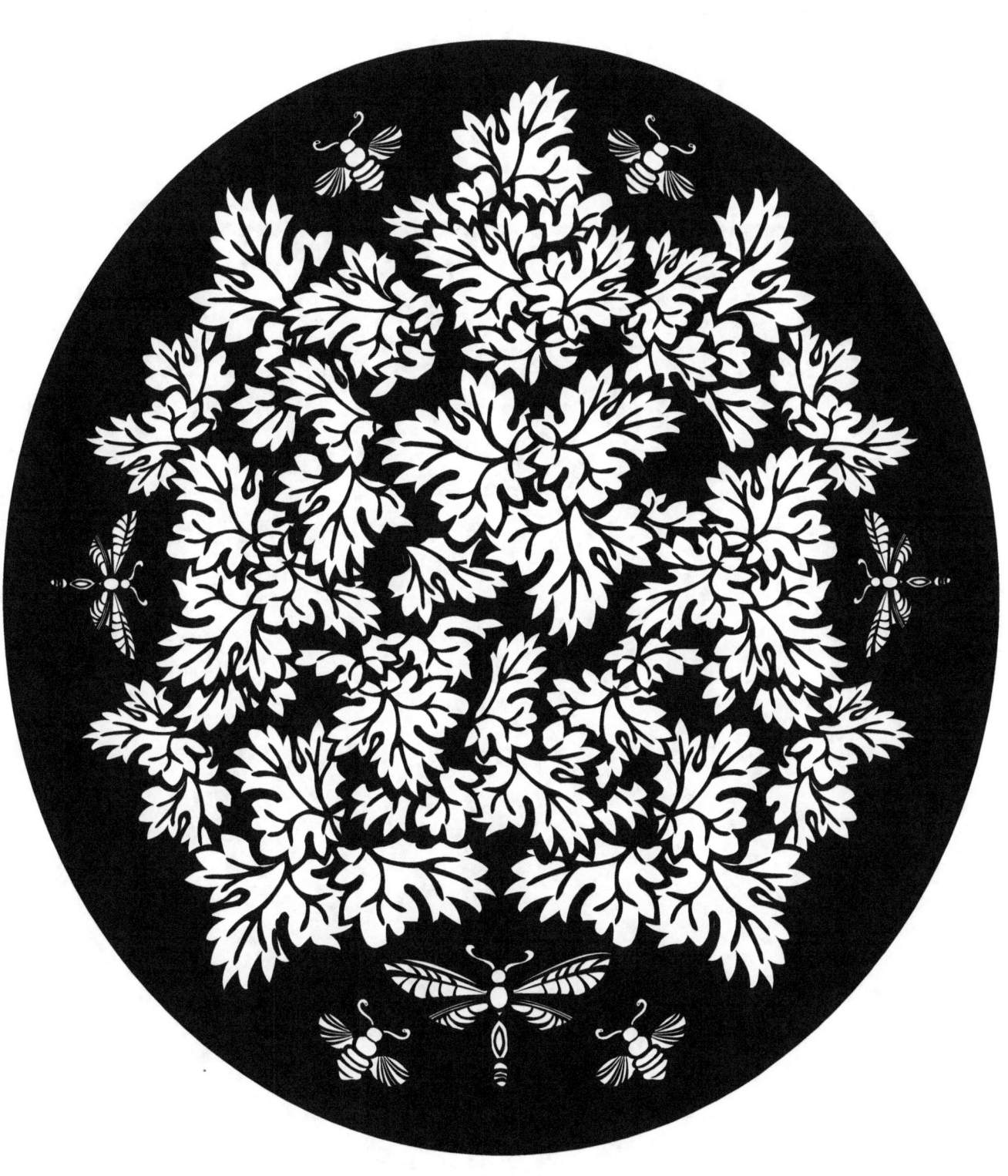

Autumn Leaves, 2015 Jennifer Kozlansky

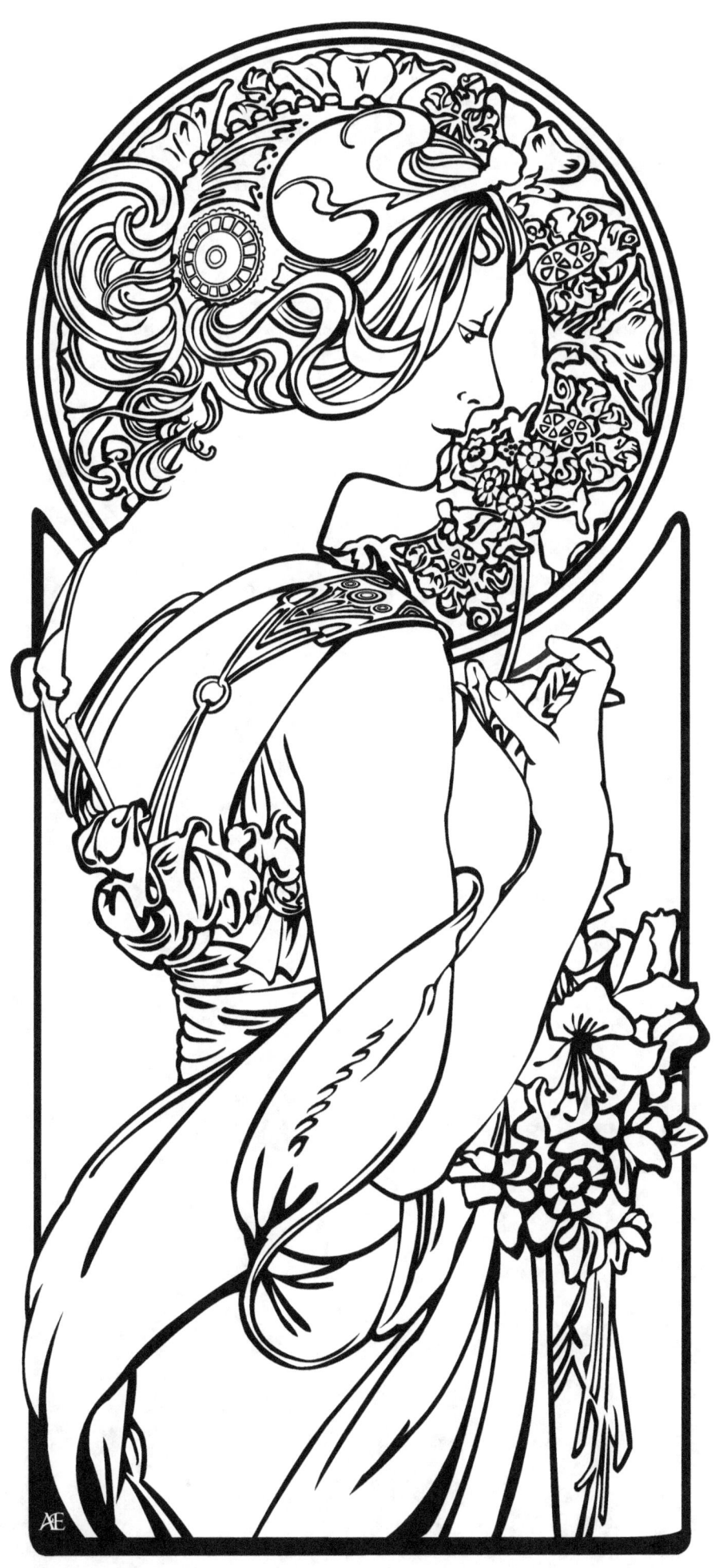

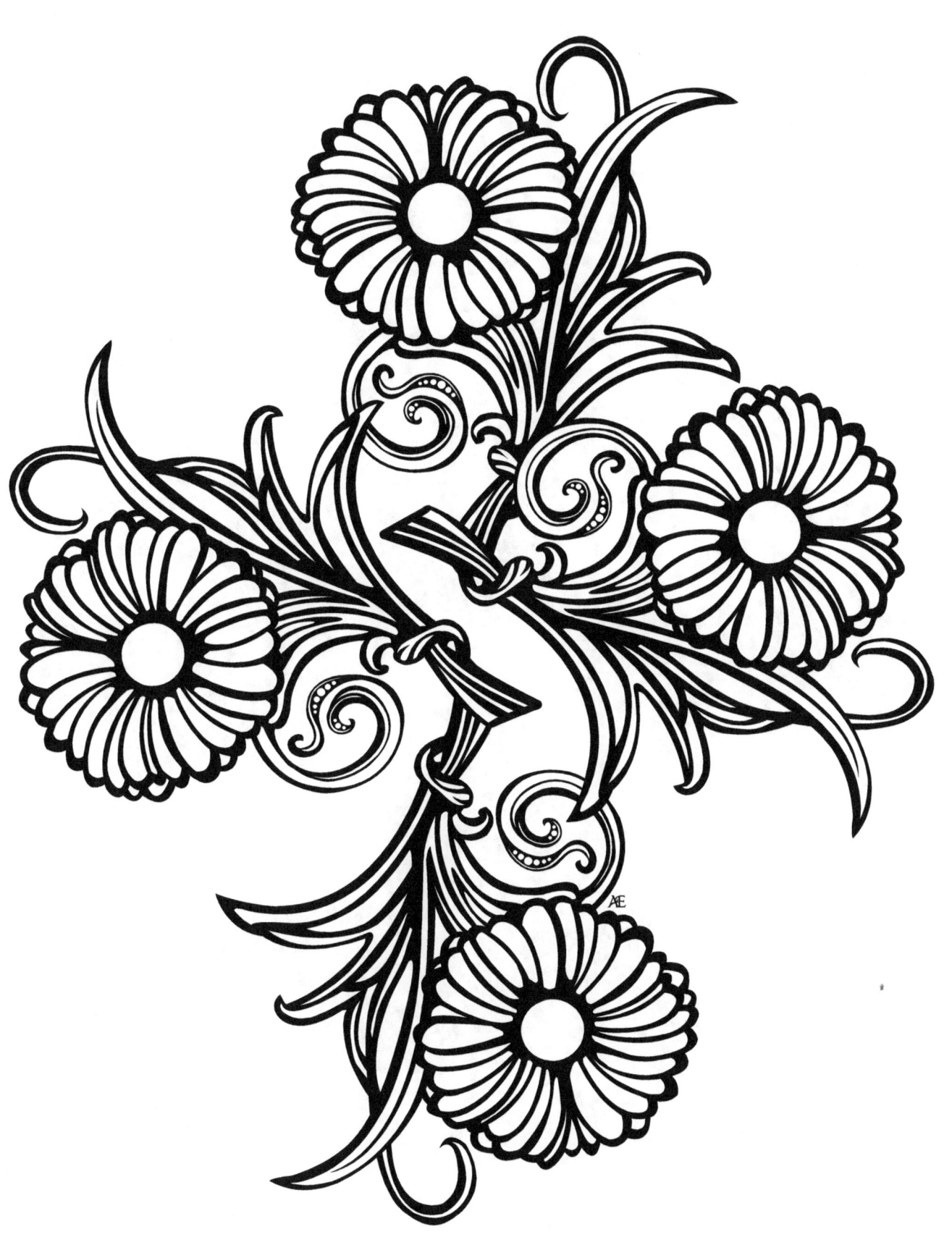

ASTERS, 2015 JENNIFER KOZLANSKY

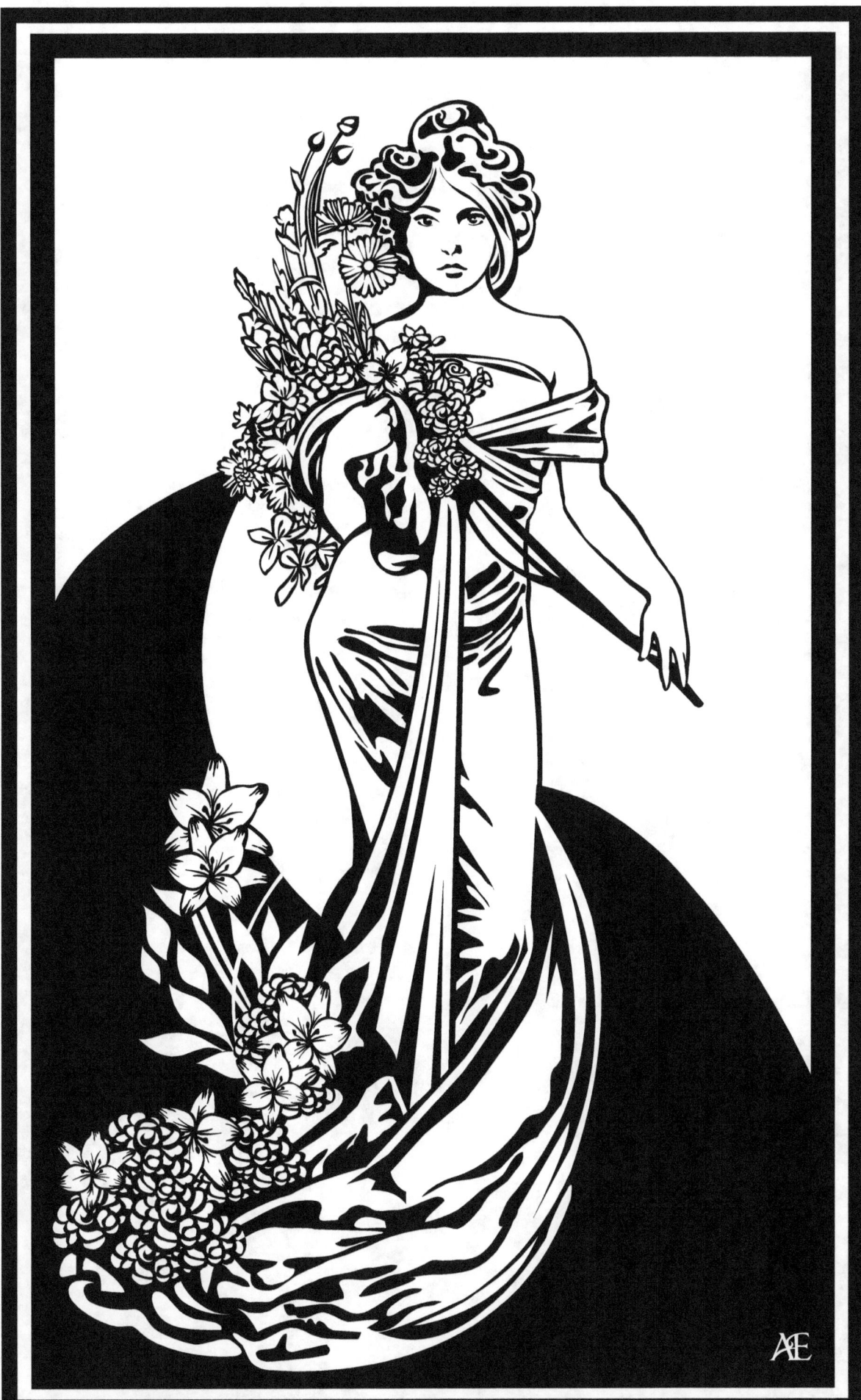

SPRING, 1900 ALPHONSE MUCHA

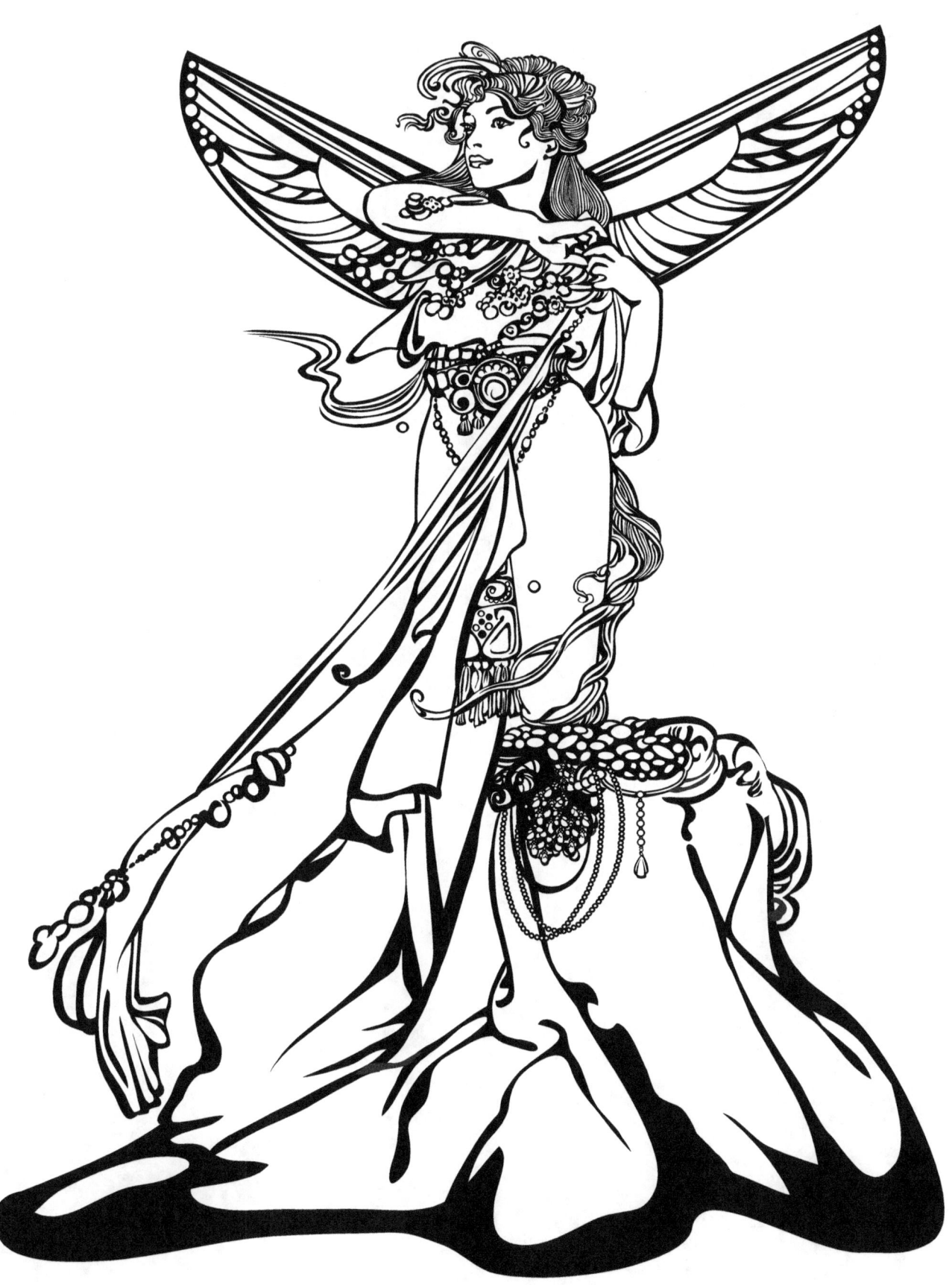

Rama, 1898 Alphonse Mucha

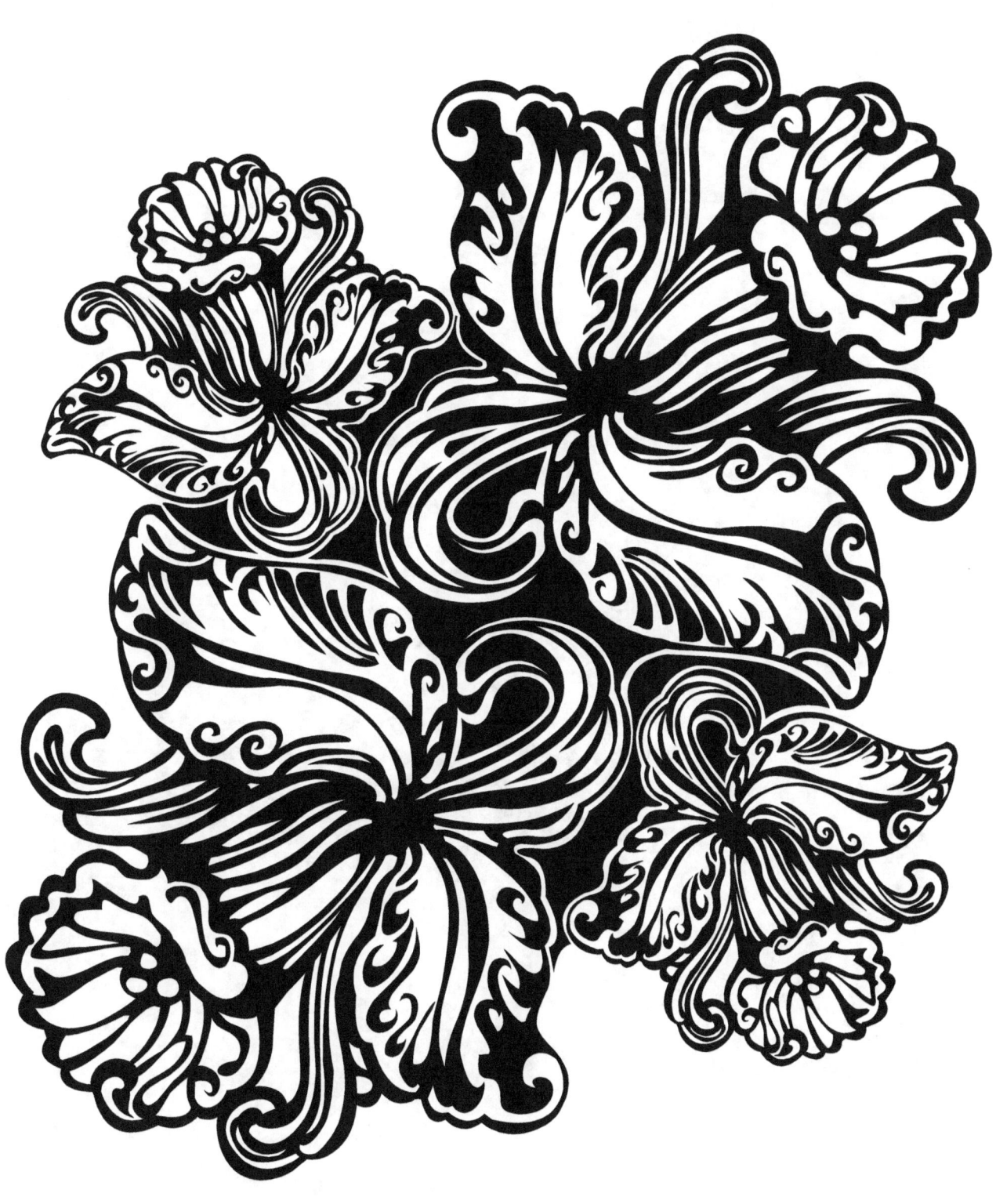

DAFFODILS, 2015 JENNIFER KOZLANSKY

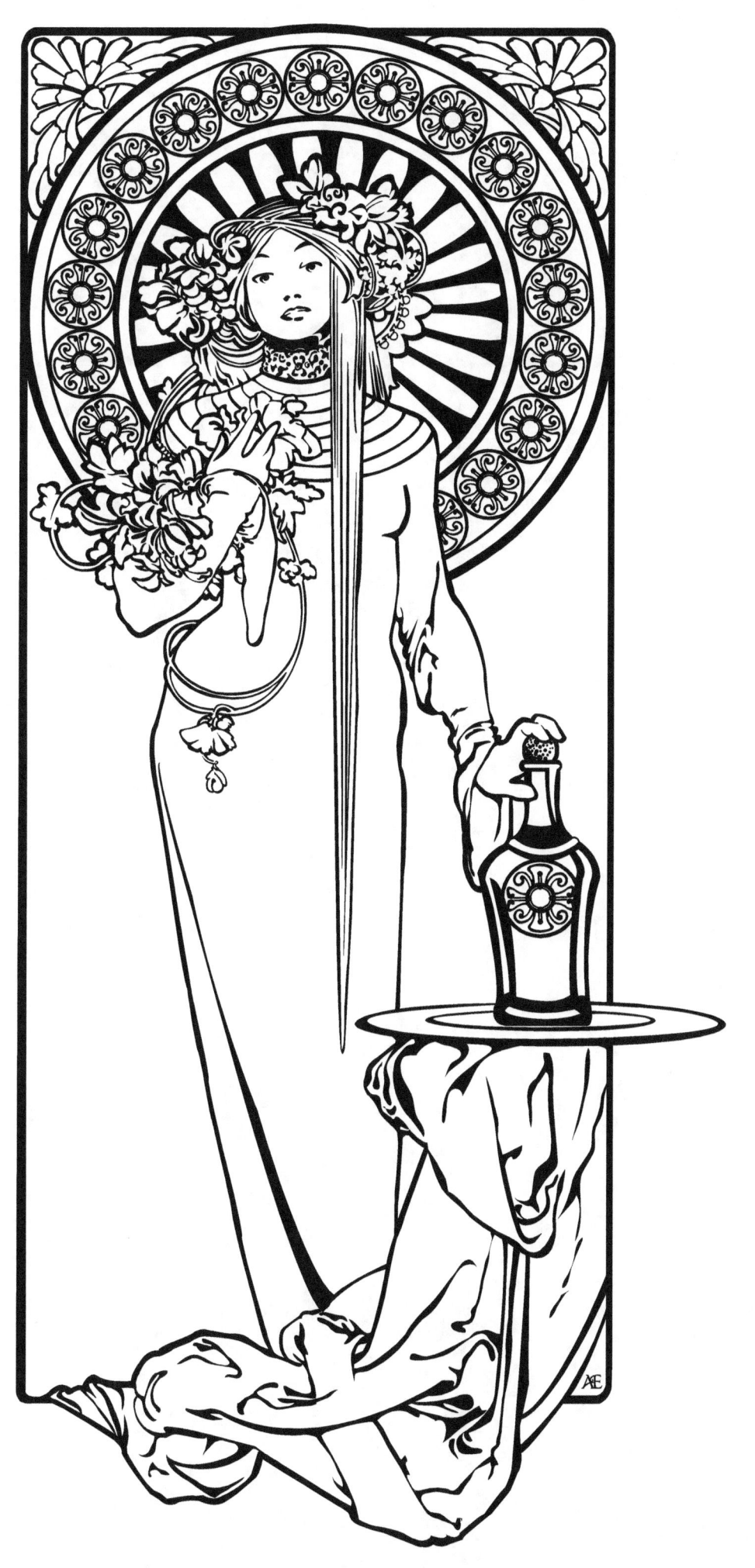

La Trappistine, 1897 Alphonse Mucha

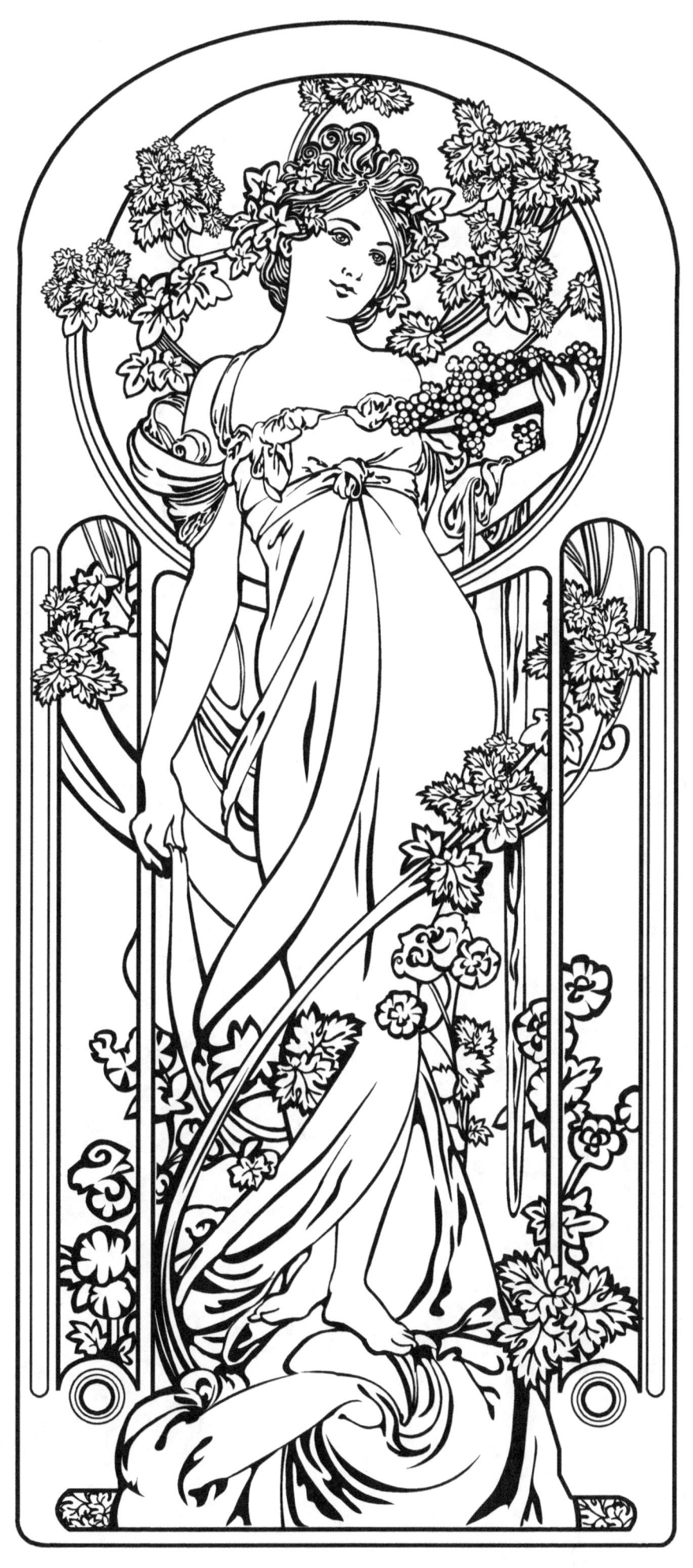

Champagne White Star, 1899 Mucha

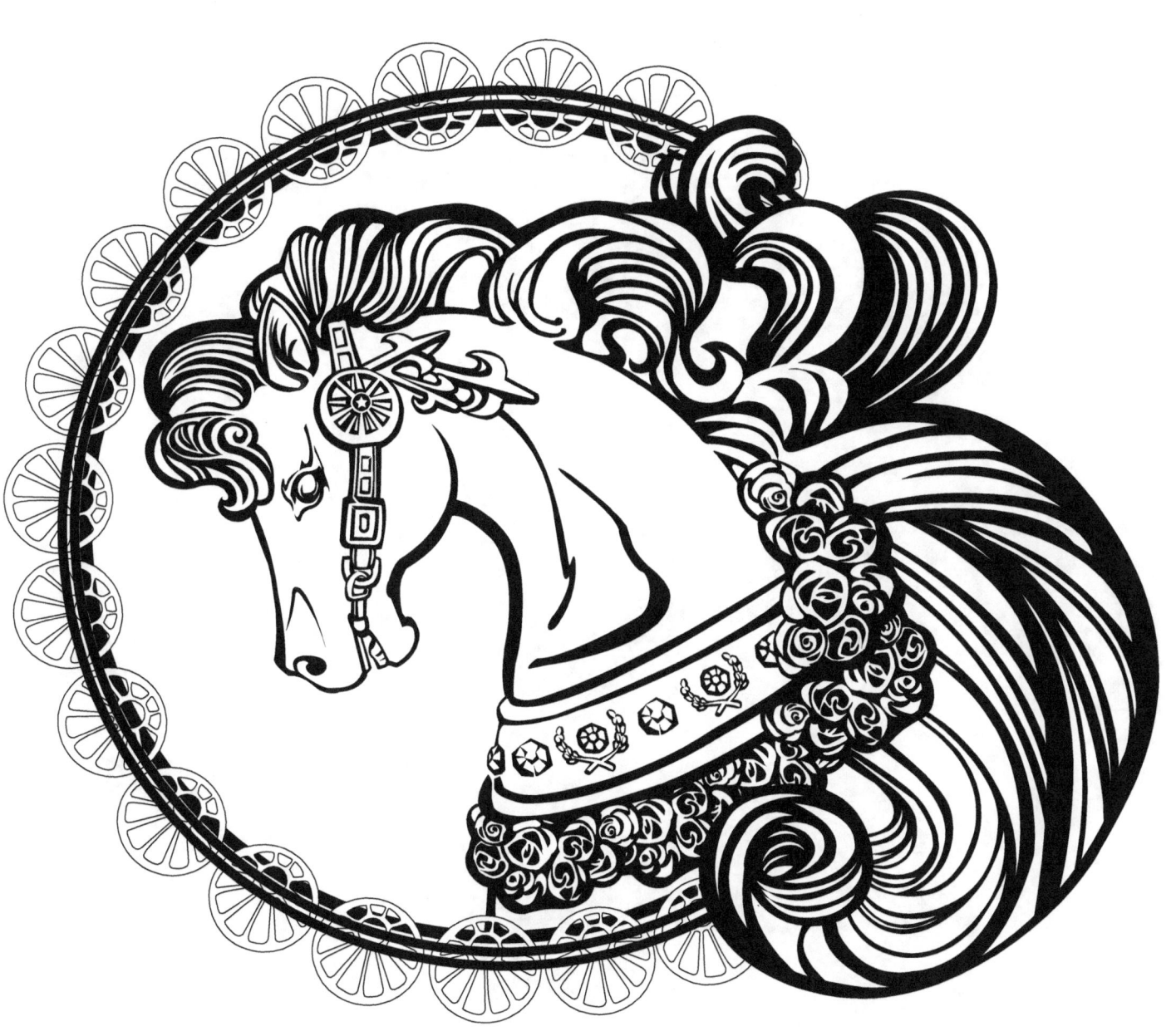

ROSE HORSE, 2015 JENNIFER KOZLANSKY

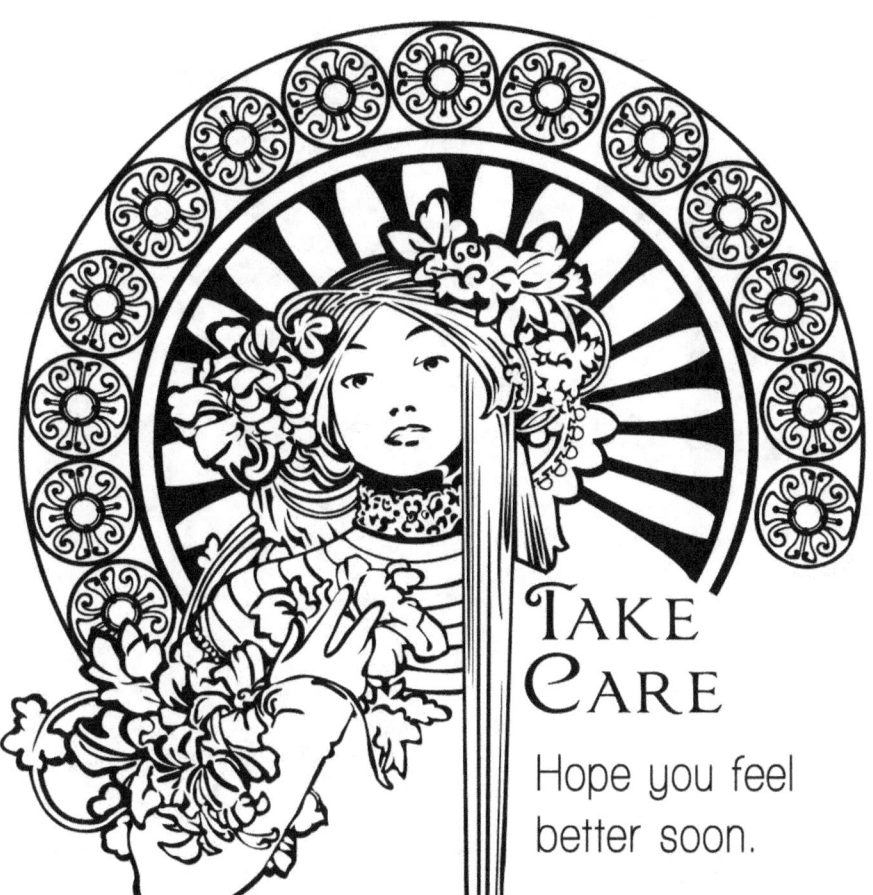

TAKE
CARE

Hope you feel
better soon.

GET WELL SENTIMENT MUCHA/KOZLANSKY

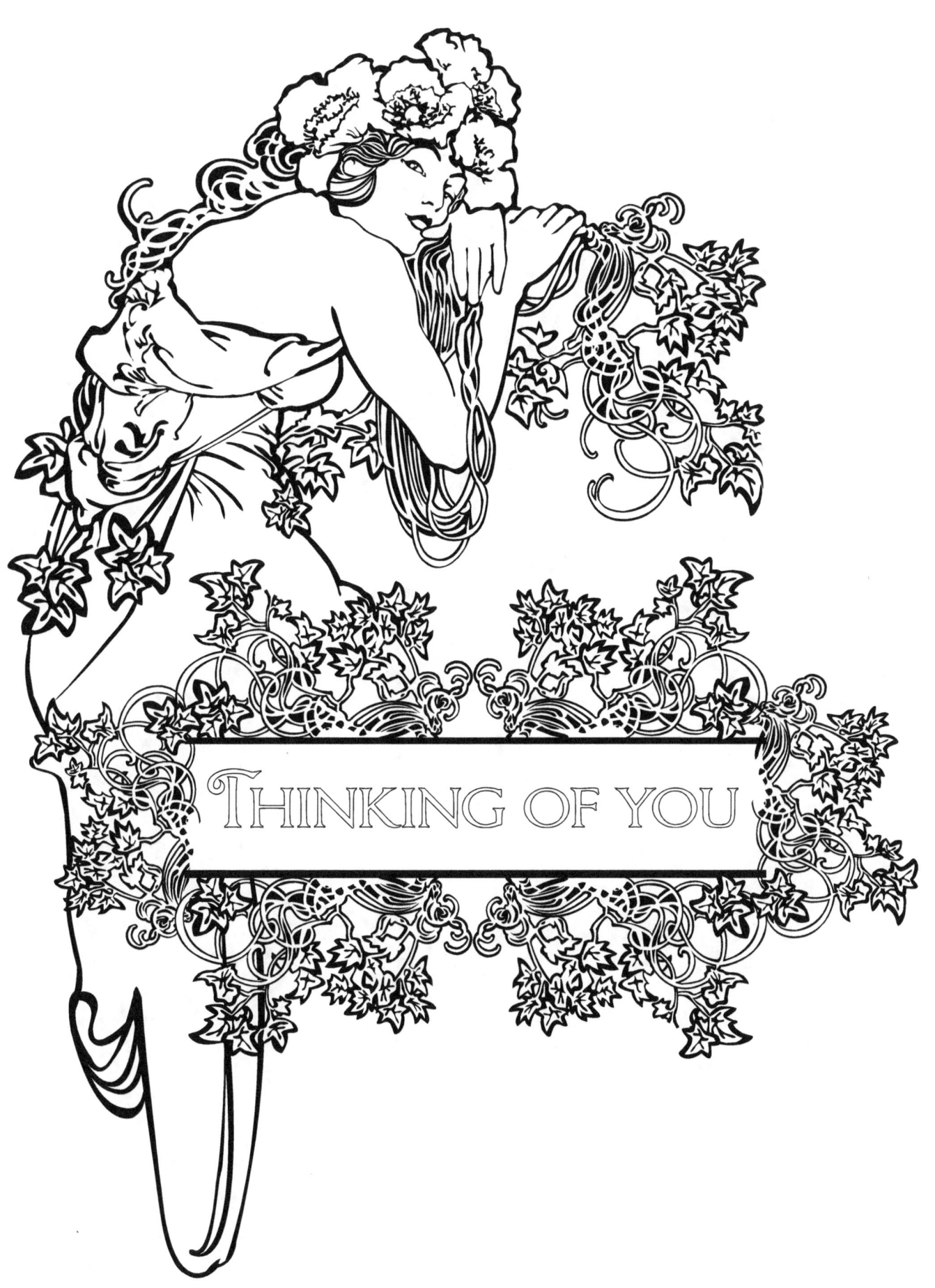

Thinking of You Sentiment Mucha/Kozlansky

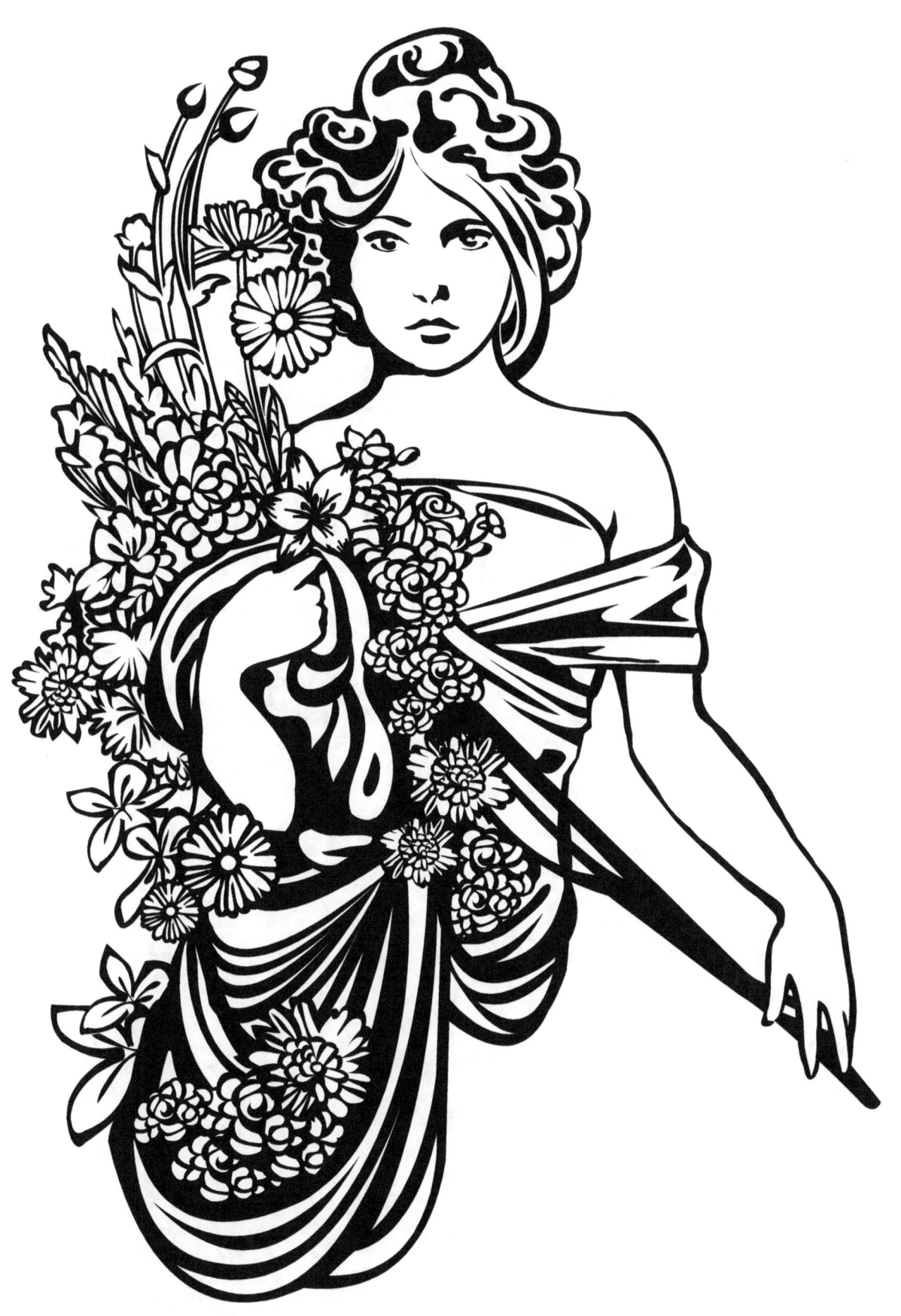

SPRING DETAIL 1900 ALPHONSE MUCHA

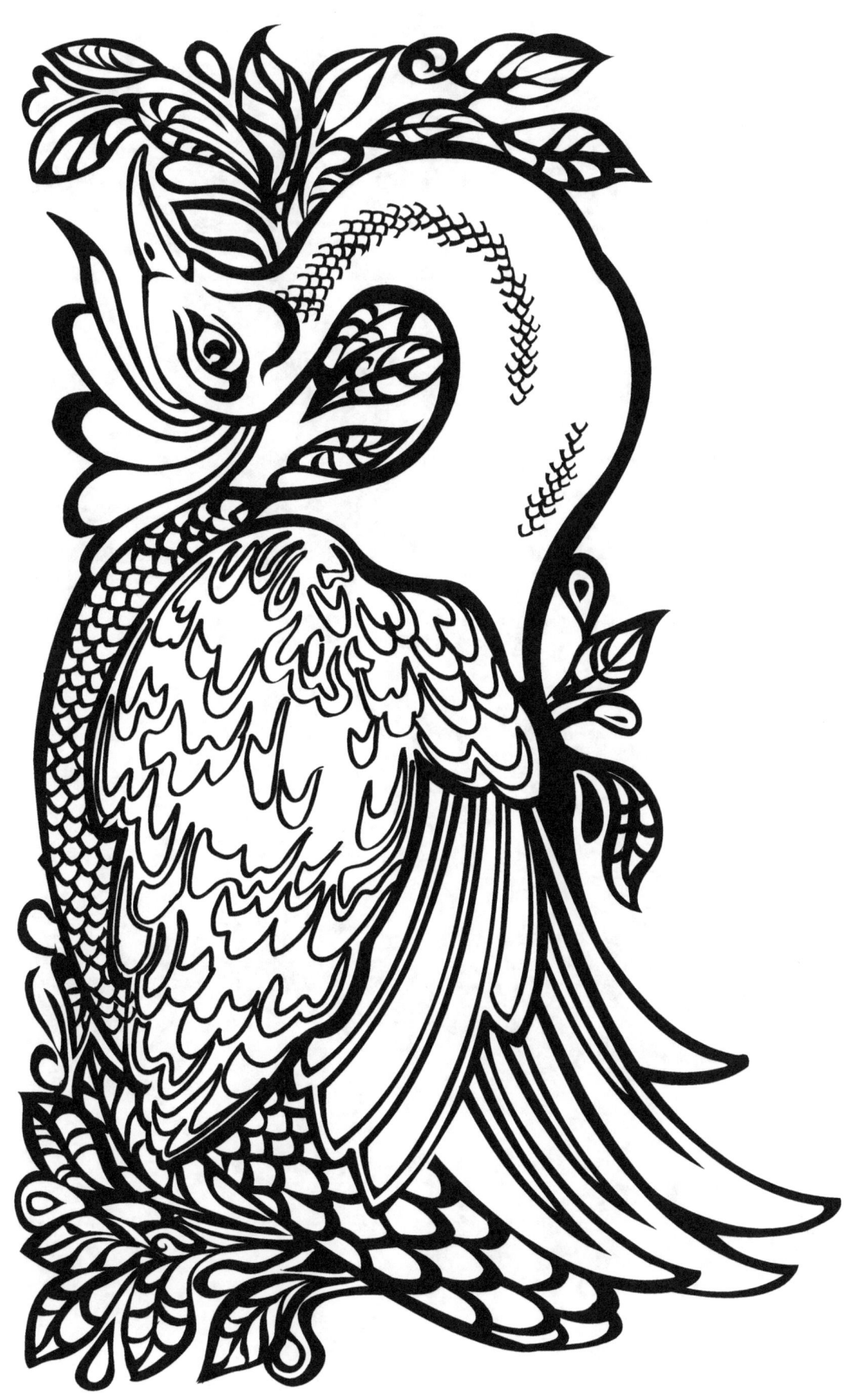

Peacock Detail 1896 A. Turbayne

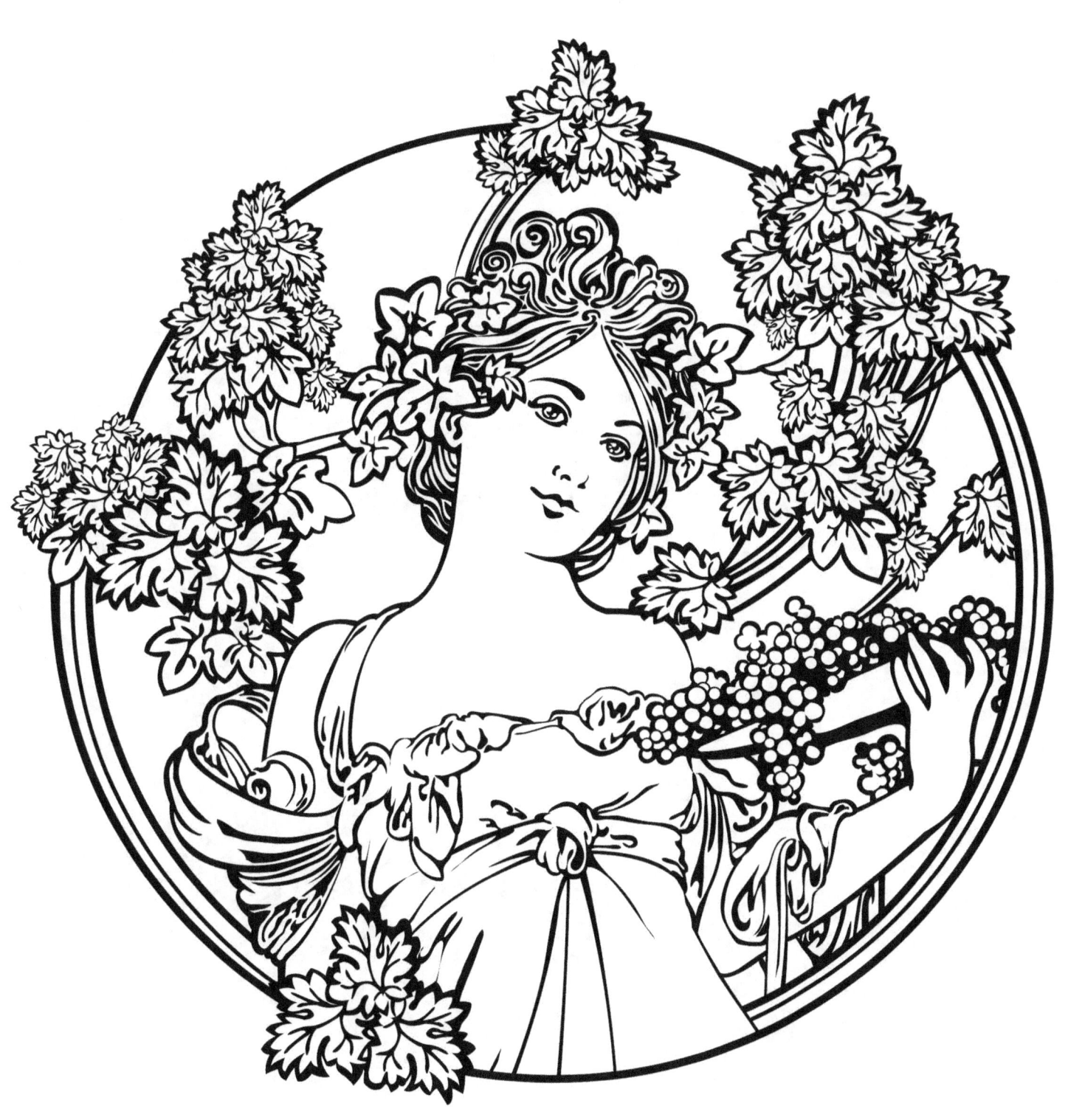

Champagne White Star Detail, 1899 Mucha

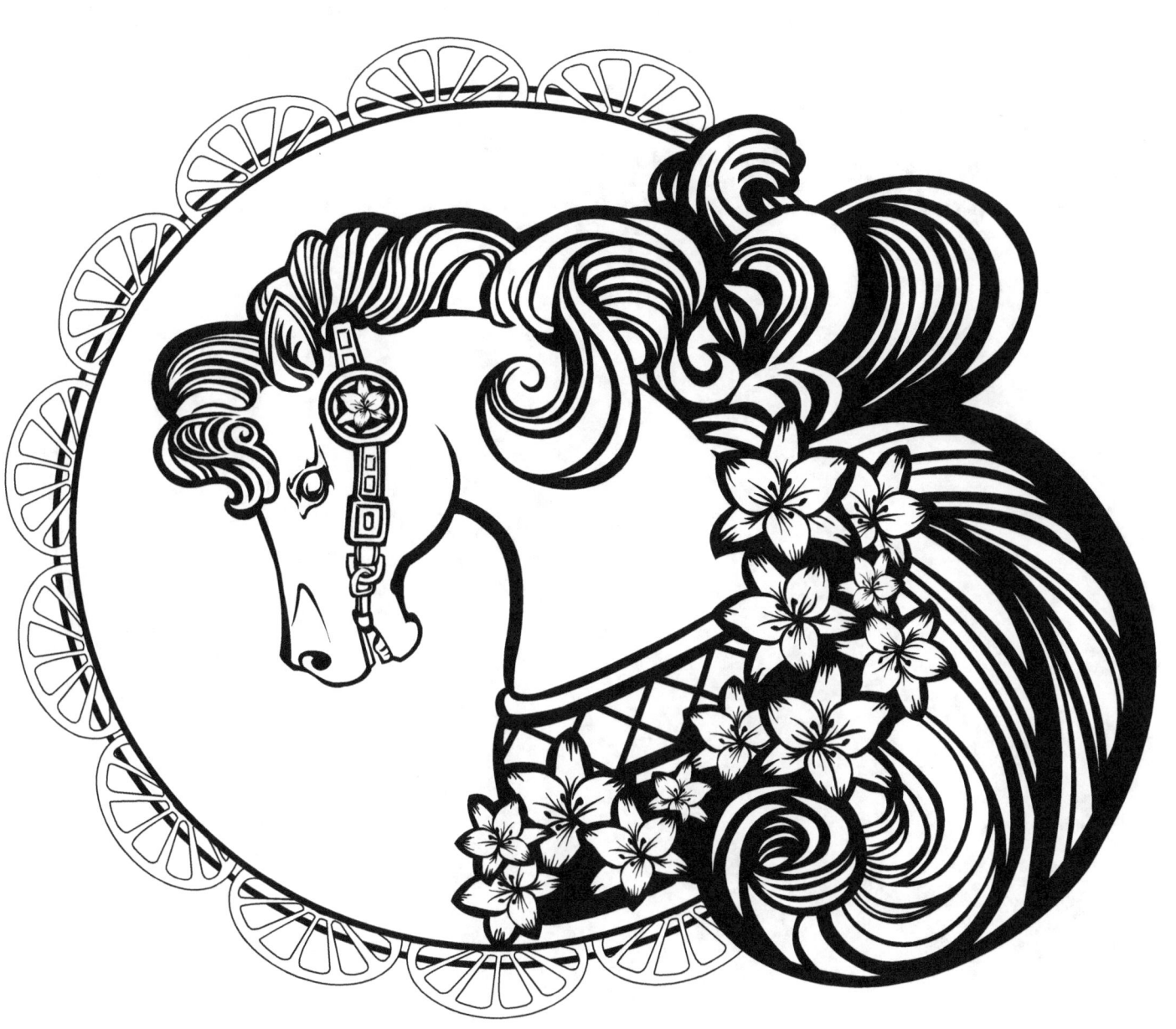

Lily Horse, 2015 Jennifer Kozlansky

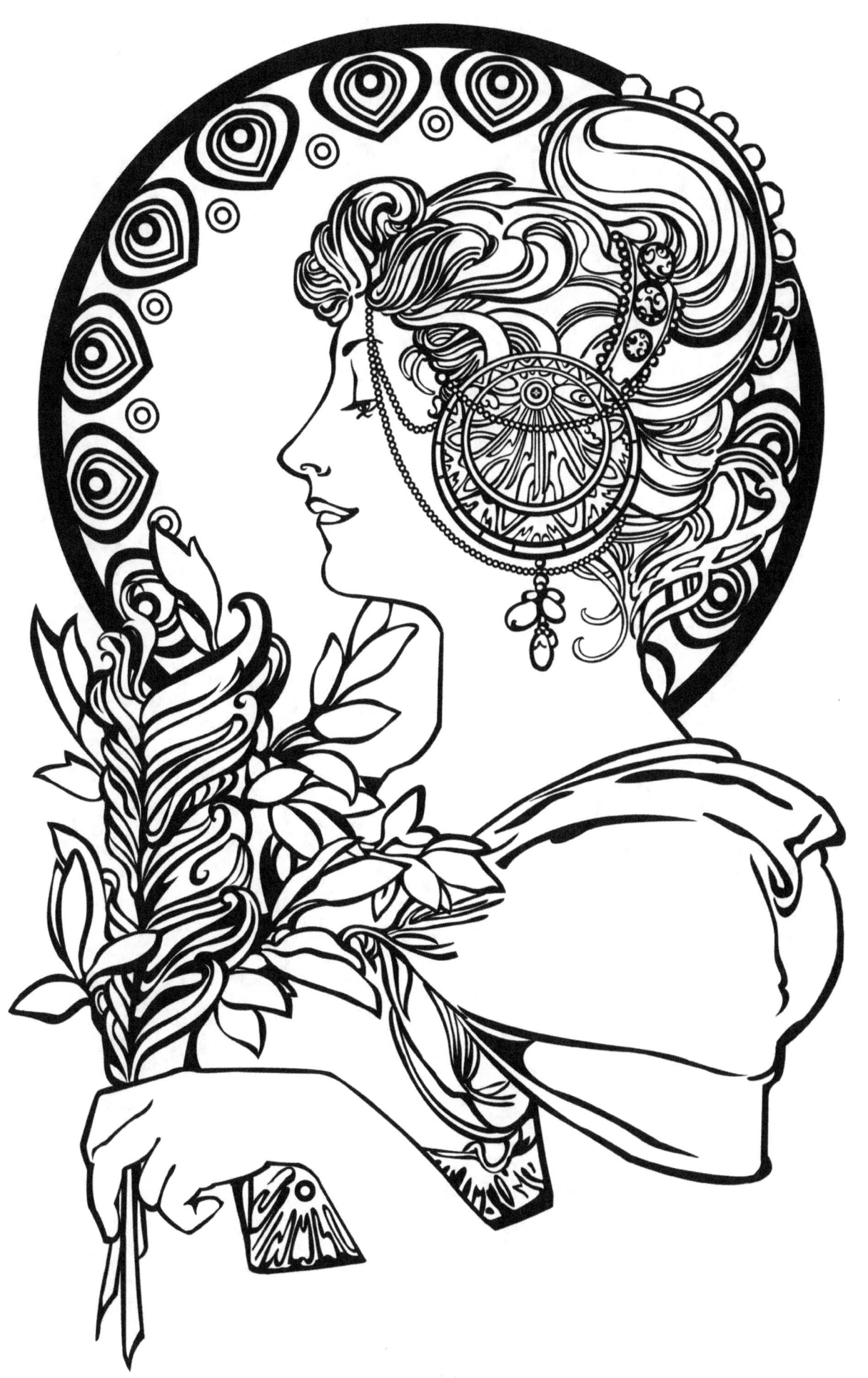

La Plume Detail 1899 Alphonse Mucha

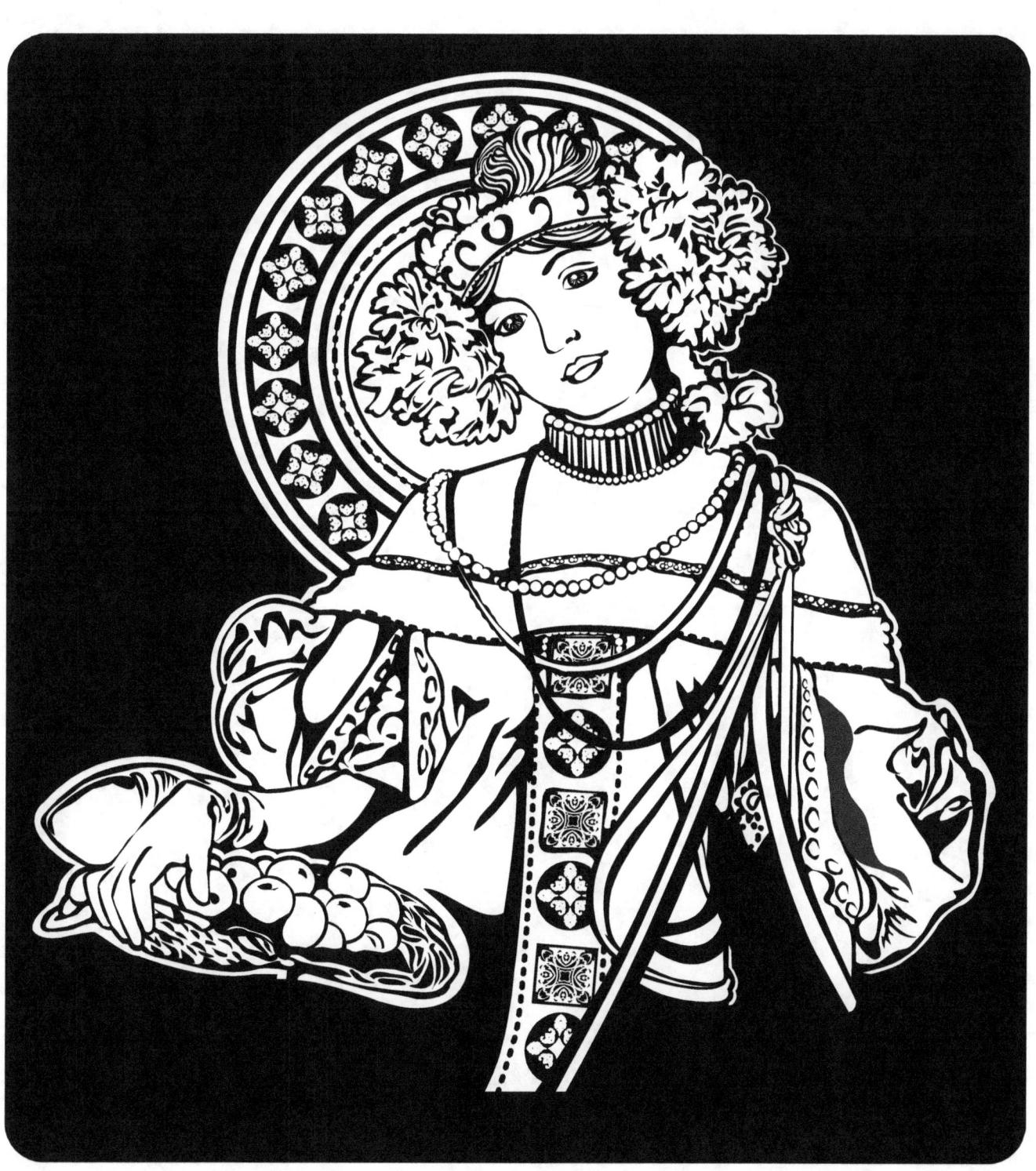

Autumn Detail 1899 Alphonse Mucha

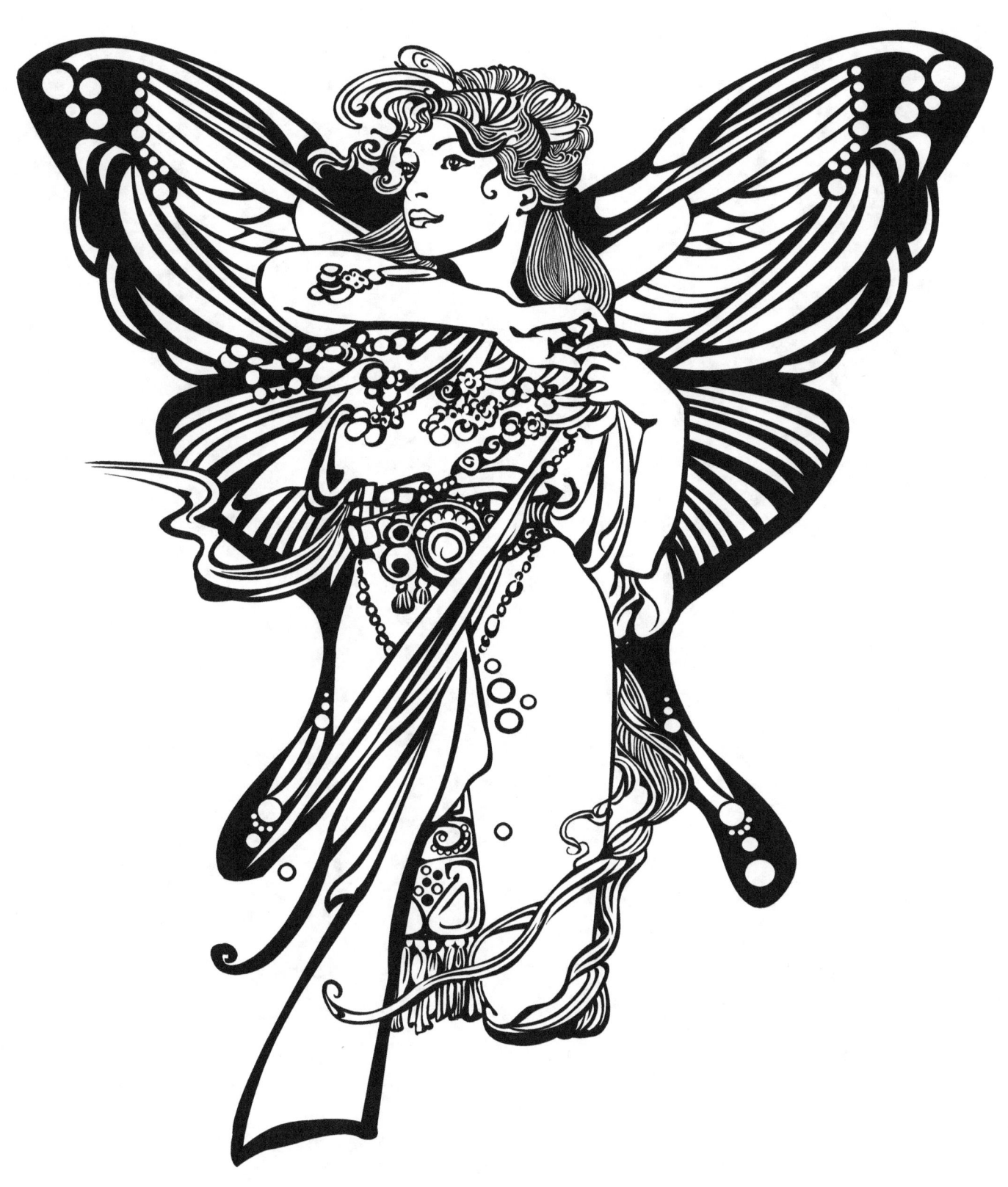

Rama "Butterfly" 1899 Mucha/Kozlansky

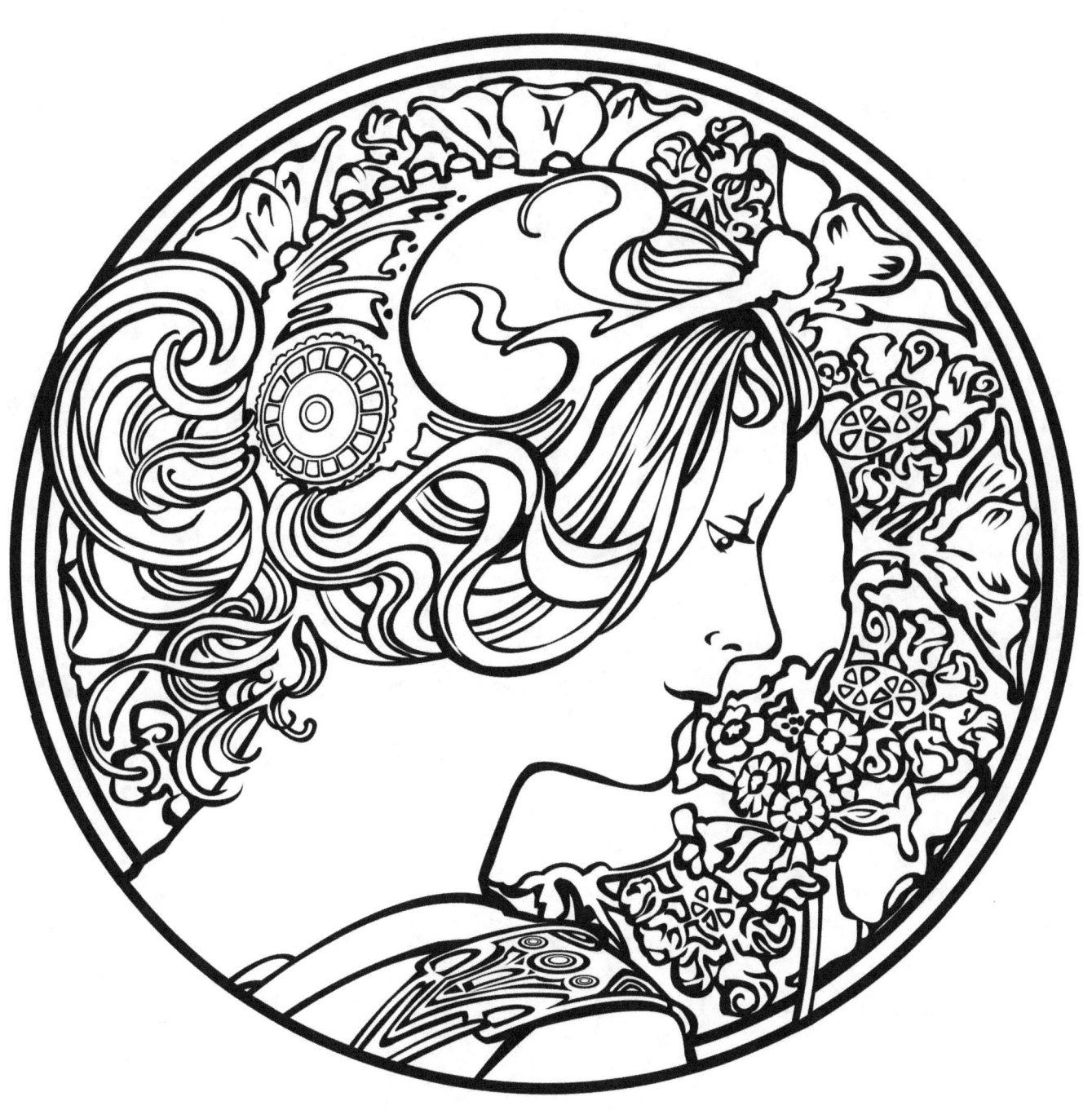

Polyanthus Detail 1899 Alphonse Mucha

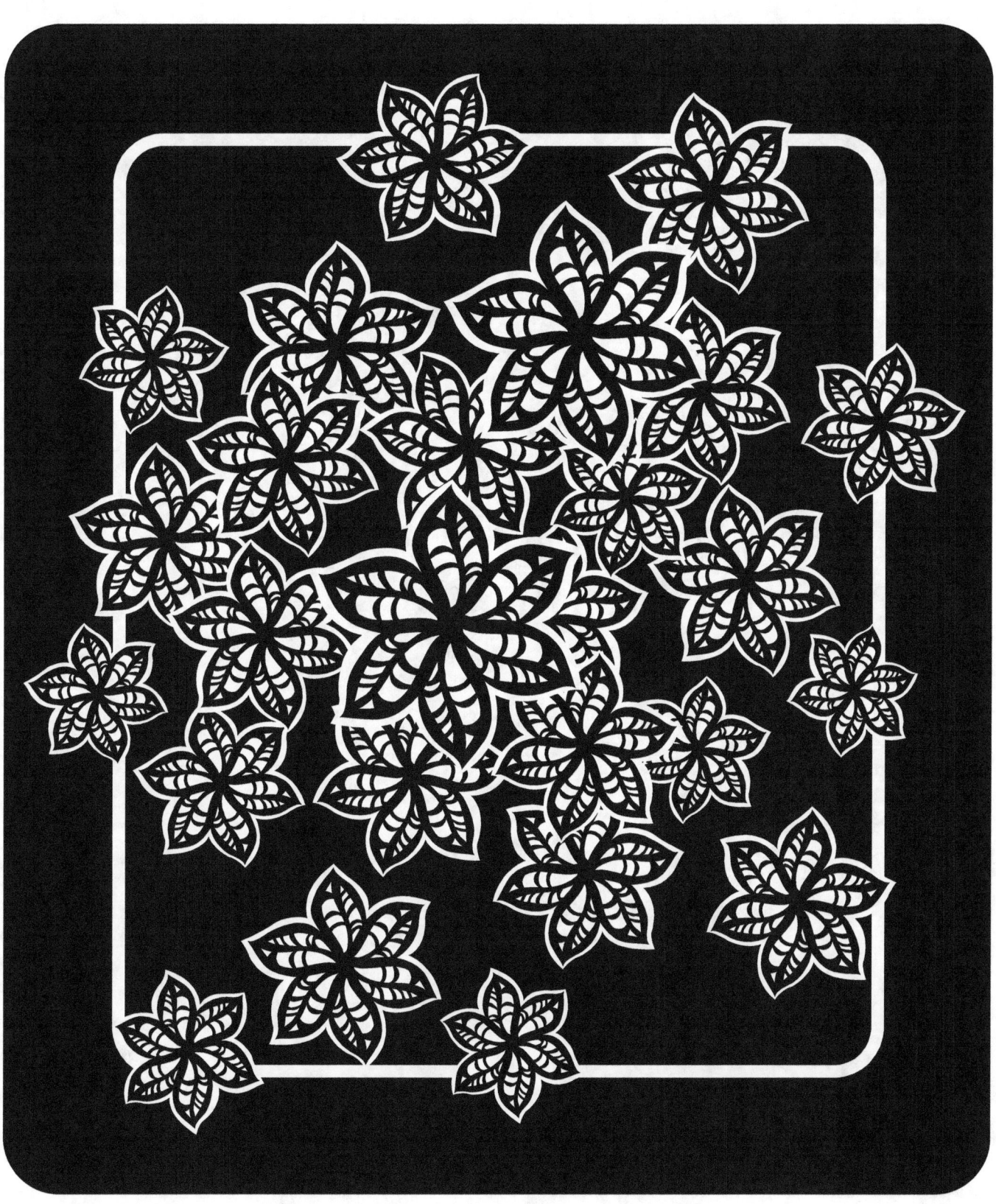

FLOWERS 2015 JENNIFER KOZLANSKY

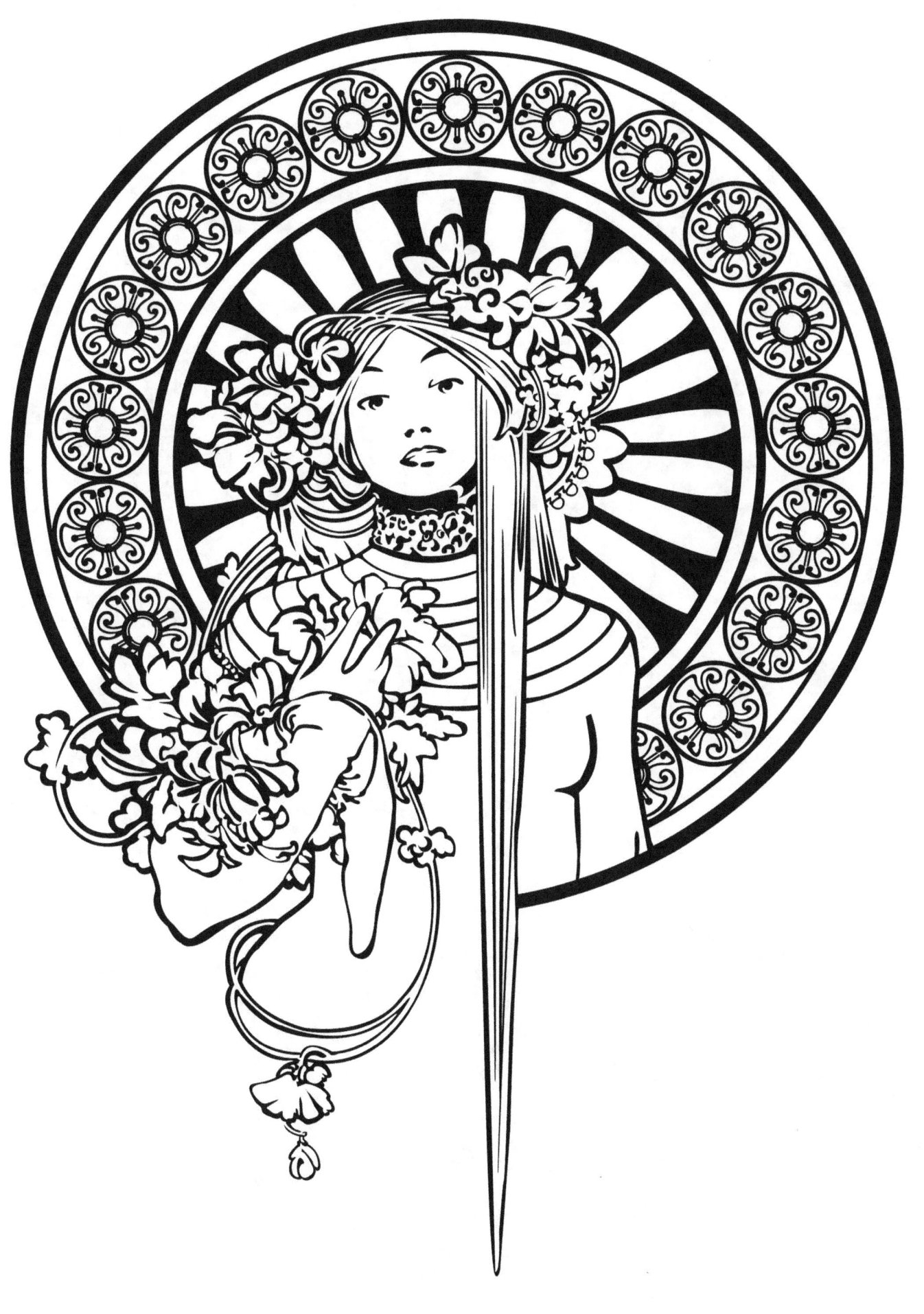

La Trappistine Detail 1897 Alphonse Mucha

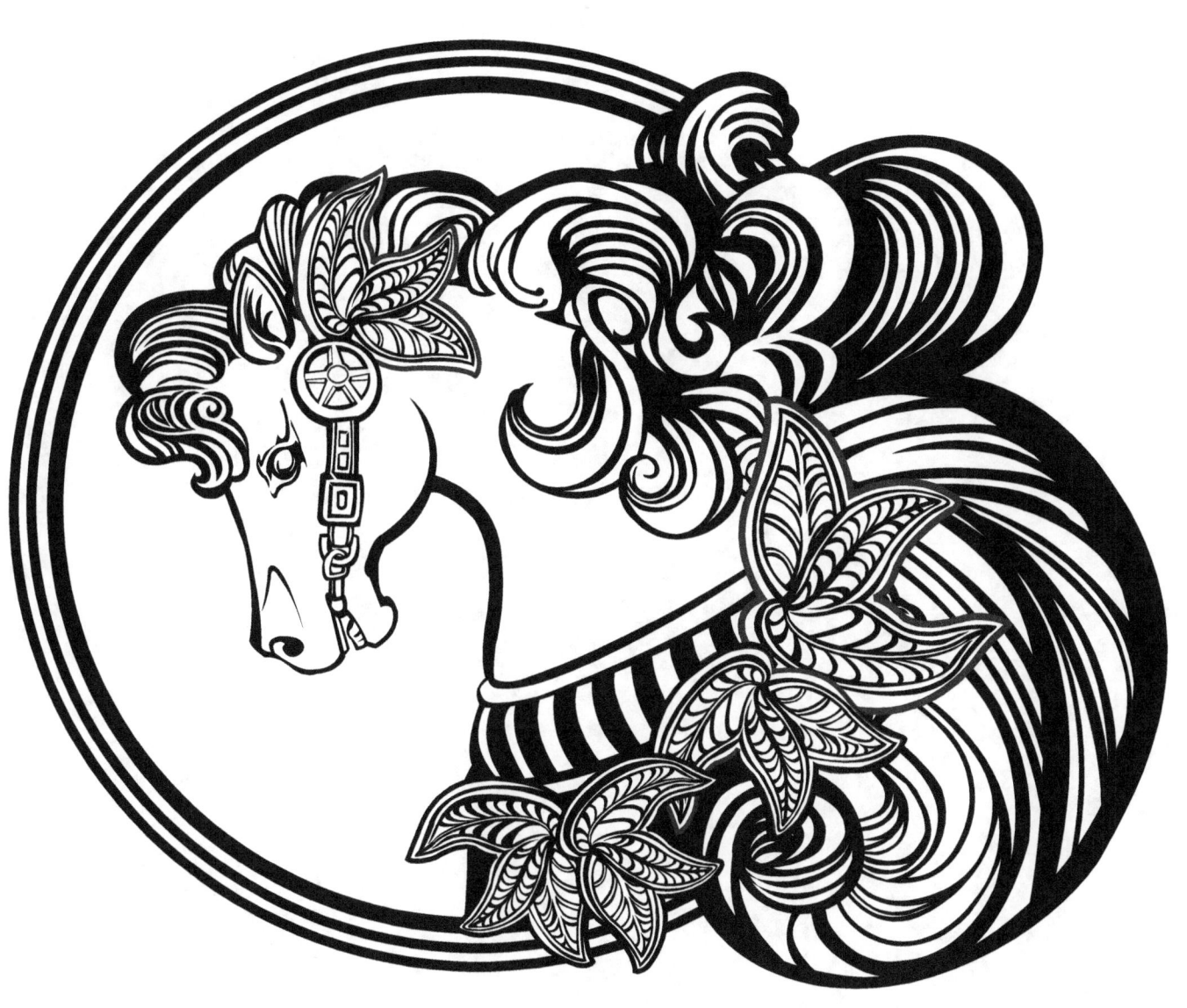

FROND HORSE 2015 JENNIFER KOZLANSKY

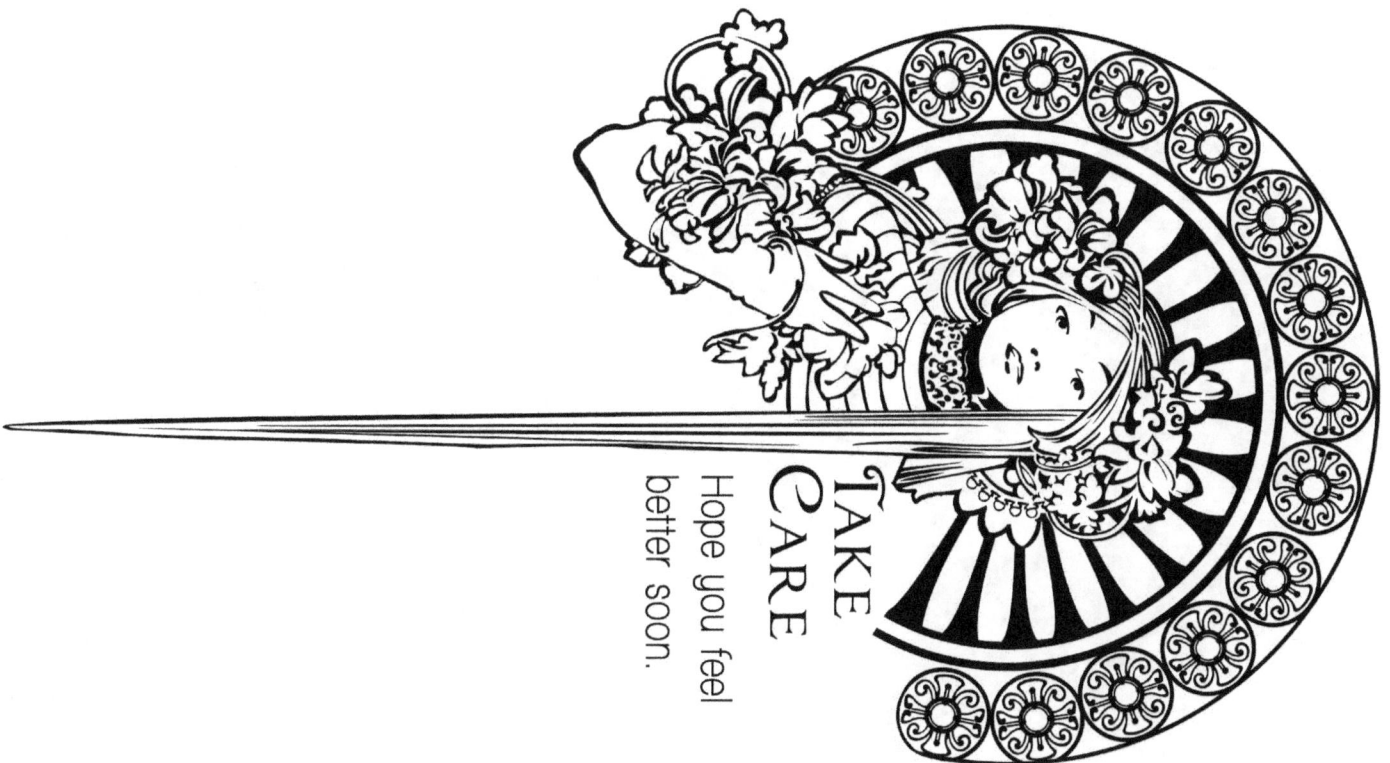

TAKE CARE

Hope you feel
better soon.

Get Well Card Mucha/Kozlansky

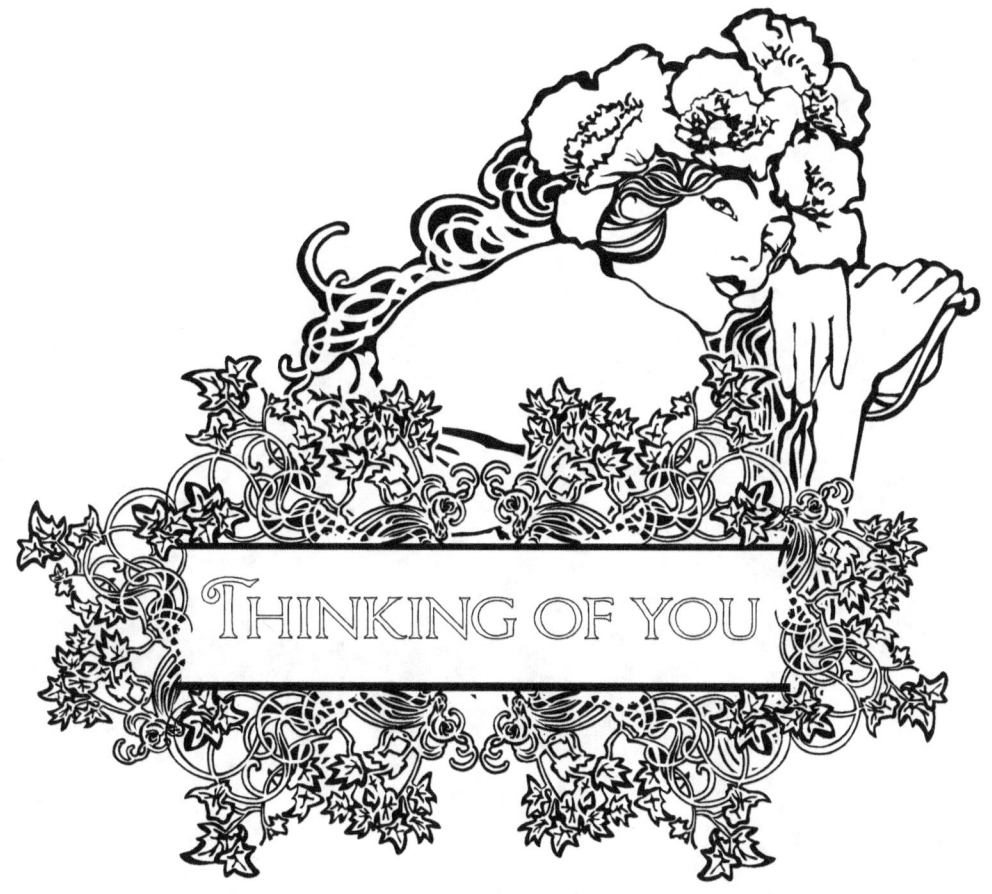

THINKING OF YOU

Thinking of You Card Mucha/Kozlansky

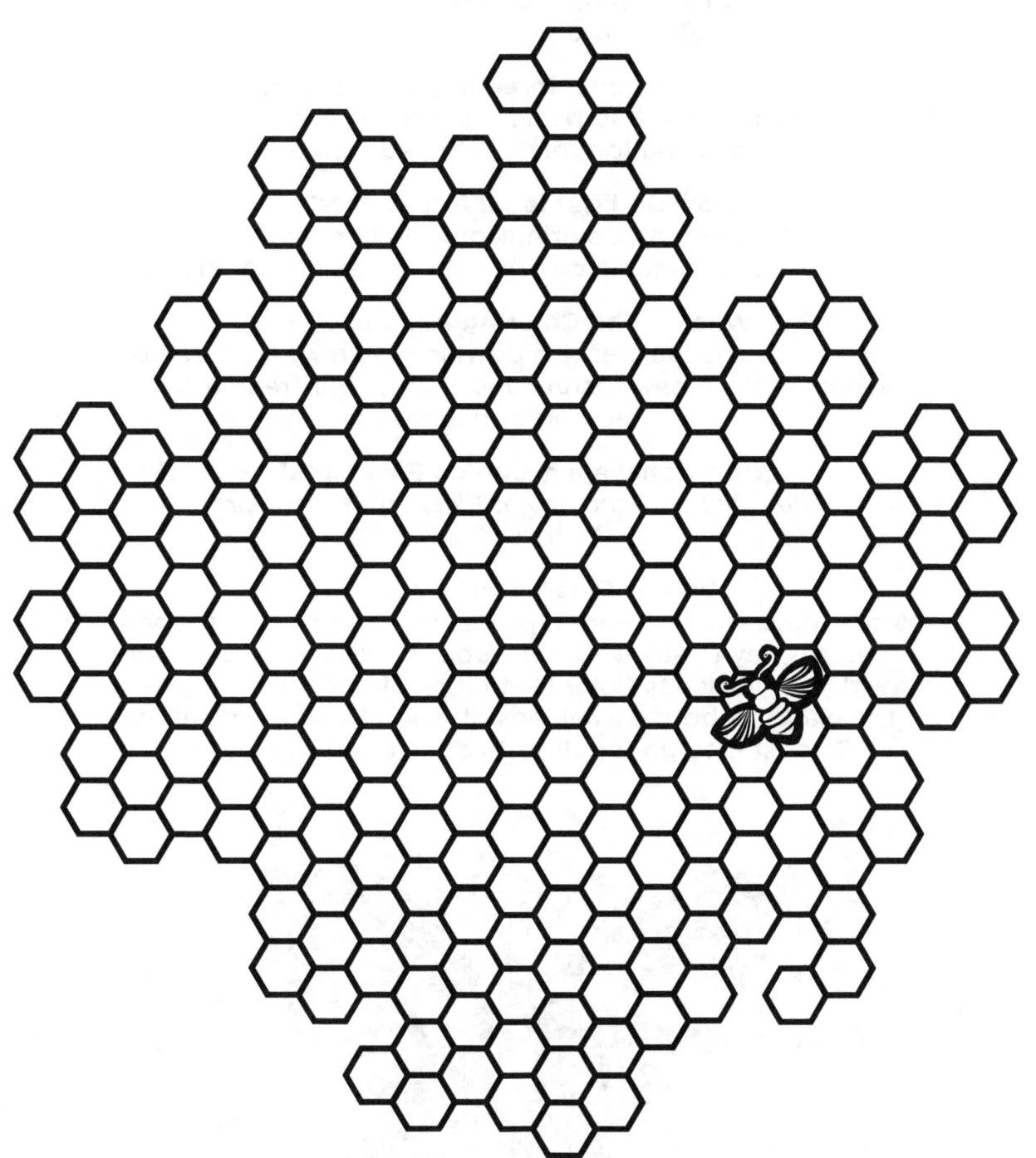

FAQ

Can I share a page I colored on Facebook?
Absolutely! Just be sure to credit FineArtColoring.com.

Can I copy uncolored pages to share?
This is illegal as it impacts the income of the artist.
Thank you for your continued support!

How do I get legal free sheets?
Sign up to FineArtColoring.com. Members get a free
coloring downloadable coloring sheet just for signing up.

What is The Coloring Academy™?
Free videos and inexpensive downloadable worksheets for
colorists to learn new techniques. Sign up for free today for
more information.

Do you have a group on Facebook?
*The Coloring Academy at FineArtColoring.com
& Colorista Corner.*

What is FineArtColoring.com?
A gorgeous line of coloring products ready to give anyone
a creative way to say *Get Well Soon*, *Thank You* or celebrate
with our gorgeous Color Party Kits. Fine Art Coloring is
the place for both casual fans of coloring and dedicated
Coloristas to go for all sorts of coloring goodness.

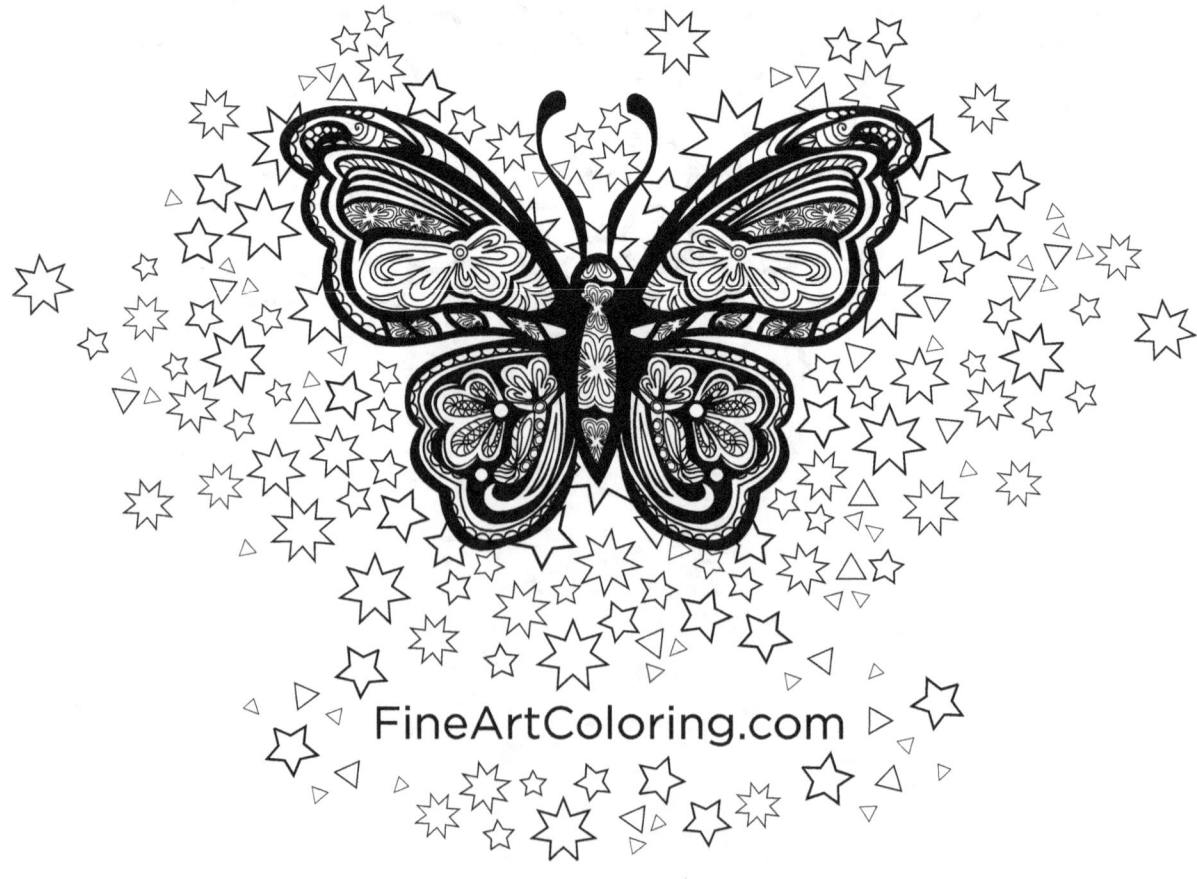

FineArtColoring.com